The Skipper's Pocketbook

Second Edition

Compiled by Basil Mosenthal
Incorporating material by
Gerry Russell, Tim Davison,
Dr Rob Haworth & David Houghton

D0865041

WILEY NAUTICAL

www.wileynautical.com

Second Edition © Fernhurst Books 2001
First Edition © Fernhurst Books 1999

Reprinted June 2008 by John Wiley & Sons Ltd
The Atrium, Southern Gate, Chichester,
West Sussex, PO19 8SQ, England.
Tel 01243 779777
Email: (For orders and customer service enquires):
cs-books@wiley.co.uk
www.wileynautical.com

Contact us for a free full-colour brochure

British Library Cataloguing in Publication Data:
A catalogue record for this book
is available from the British Library

ISBN 978 1 898 66078 1

Printed in China through World Print

Cover design by Simon Balley
Designed by Creative Byte

The author and publisher gratefully acknowledge the assistance
given by Pains Wessex p.16, J Michael Gale (Pan Pan call) p.19,
Simpson-Lawrence (anchor table) p.75, Steve Judkins and Tim
Davison's book *Knots & Splices* p.95-6, Volvo Penta UK Ltd
(diagrams) p.100-104, Pat Manley (engine data), RYA (weather
map) p81, and pp 84,88.

The following are reproduced from Admiralty Charts and
Publications with the permission of the Controller of Her
Majesty's Stationery Office, the United Kingdom Hydrographic
Office: chart p.28, symbols pp.30,31, Dover curve p.39,
Devonport data p.40, curve p.41, Solent curve p.42, tidal
chart and stream data p.43, Tidal Stream & Computation of
Rates table p.44. The form of many of these is from The
MacMillan Nautical Almanac, which is gratefully acknowledged.
Cover photos courtesy of Plastimo (compass),
Gary John Norman (rope).

RYA and YACHTMASTER are registered trade marks of the Royal Yachting Association

Introduction

It is easy to take for granted how much a good yacht skipper needs to know. Navigation, finding the way into a new harbour, using the radio correctly, checking the engine, noting something aloft that may need repair, reading the weather forecast wisely – all these things and many more can be part of a skipper's day.

But skippers are busy people. Details are easily overlooked, and reminders are always useful. This pocketbook is not a textbook, but an invaluable aide-memoire of much that a skipper needs to know – both to look after his boat and sail her safely.

It should also prove an invaluable reference book for the RYA® Yachtmaster® syllabus. We all need to 'sail safely'. As a result of working with the RNLI and the Coastguard the book not only shows how to deal with emergencies but also how to prevent things going wrong in the first place.

With this book in your pocket, I hope you will have many happy hours afloat.

Basil Mosenthal

Contents

Sailing safely

WHAT GOES WRONG

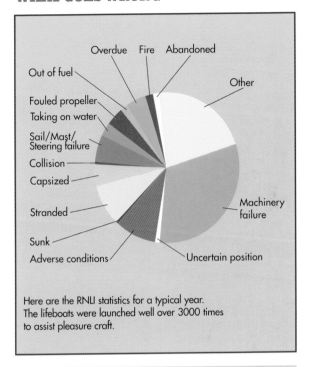

Overdue Fire Abandoned

Out of fuel

Fouled propeller
Taking on water
Sail/Mast/
Steering failure
Collision
Capsized
Stranded
Sunk
Adverse conditions

Other

Machinery
failure

Uncertain position

Here are the RNLI statistics for a typical year.
The lifeboats were launched well over 3000 times
to assist pleasure craft.

READY FOR SEA?

- What is the weather forecast?
- Engine has been checked and run.
- Fuel checked and enough for the passage.
- Emergency equipment checked recently (when?).
- VHF radio checked.
- GPS set up (if being used).
- Tide and tidal streams noted in the log.
- Crew briefed as necessary (including knowing how to reef).
- Compass and navigation lights tested (if any chance of
  being out after dark).
- Gear secure on and below decks, including galley.
- Hatches and ports closed.
- Bilges dry (has anyone looked?).
- Standing rigging looked over. Mainsail reefing set up.
- Sails ready for hoisting when needed.
- Does anyone know where you are going and when
  you expect to arrive or return to harbour?
- Can the crew cope?

MAN OVERBOARD - PREVENTION

The important issue is to prevent anyone ever going overboard.

Lifelines
- Minimum height for top lifeline (guardrail) is 60 cm (24"), and 66 cm (26") is better. The lower lifeline should be at least 23 cm (9") above deck to prevent anyone sliding under the top rail.
- Although the lower lifeline should be low enough to prevent anyone sliding under it, a toe-rail not less than 25 mm high is an added safeguard.

Harnesses
- Each crew member must have a safety harness, adjusted to fit and stowed with their personal gear.
- A crutch strap is recommended.
  The European standard for harnesses is EN1095.
- Two lanyards are best - a short one of around a metre and a longer one of two metres, which can also be elasticated. Having two lanyards has a great advantage when moving around. One is always clipped on while the other is changed. Use the short one in the cockpit for greater security.

Adjust harness

Fit to oilskins

Clipping on
- Whenever possible clip on to a point to windward.
- Any strong point used for clipping on must be through-bolted with large backing plates.
- Never clip to lifelines (guardrails) or running rigging.
- Crew coming on deck from below must be able to clip on before leaving the companionway (an eye at the fore end of the cockpit works well). Then, when settled in the cockpit, the lanyard can be transferred.
- Use jackstays when leaving the cockpit.
- On motor yachts clip on to a point near the centreline because the high speed makes falling overboard especially dangerous.

WIND

Clip to windward using jackstays

Wearing safety harnesses - the rules
- There must be firm rules for wearing harnesses.

Normally
- always on deck at night
- always in heavy weather
- always by new crew when on the foredeck
- by non-swimmers at all times.

- This must be accepted as a matter of routine, and never queried or discussed.
- No one, especially the young, should be allowed to feel that it is 'macho' not to wear a harness when required, and any older or more cautious crew member must never be ridiculed for wearing a harness (or a lifejacket) when it may not seem strictly necessary.

OTHER DECK SAFETY

Slipping
- Use proper deck shoes or boots.
- Fit treads to hatches and coachroof.

Main boom
- Control the mainsheet when gybing.

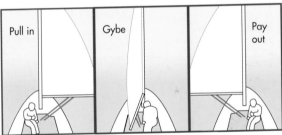

Pull in   Gybe   Pay out

- Control the boom when hoisting and lowering the mainsail.
- Fit a preventer when running.

Reefing
- Practise reefing in calm conditions.

The dinghy
- Be careful in the tender (dinghy). Don't overcrowd the boat, carry oars, enough fuel and a torch. Use lifejackets in marginal conditions.

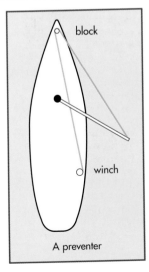

A preventer

Radar Reflector

- Octagonal reflectors, minimum diameter 45 cm (18"), must be mounted in the 'catch rain' position.

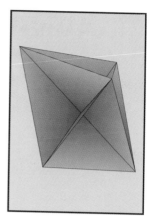

- Radar Target Enhancers are easy to mount and 'magnify' the signal.
- The minimum effective height is 4 metres (13').

FIRE PREVENTION

The main risks are petrol, gas - and smokers!

Petrol engines

- Always run the extractor fan before starting the engine.
- Keep a constant lookout for leaking fuel lines.
- Check that the fuel filling point on deck is electrically bonded to the fuel tank.

Outboards

- Store on deck (usually on the pushpit).
- Spare fuel carried on deck, or in a proper gas locker that vents overboard. Do not stow in any other locker below decks.

Gas

- Store cylinders in a proper locker, with a drain overboard.
- Secure the cylinders upright.
- The piping to the stove must be professionally fitted copper or stainless steel tubing.
- Fit an audible alarm in the deepest part of the bilge.
- Turn off the gas at the cylinder when not in use.

Escape hatches

- Make sure people can escape from forward and aft cabins.

GALLEY

- The stove must have a fixed fiddle. The kettle and pots must fit inside it.
- Lock the gimbals when opening the oven door or the stove will keel over, tipping the pots off the top.
- Fit a crash bar to prevent the cook falling onto the stove, and a cook's belt to hold him in place.
- The cook must wear protection on legs and feet to prevent burns when the boat lurches. (Oilskin trousers in rough weather.)

2 Dealing with emergencies

READY FOR AN EMERGENCY?

- LIFERAFT
  Servicing in date - securely stowed - inflating lanyard secured.

- LIFEJACKETS
  Enough for all crew - stowed to be quickly accessible
  - air bottles (where fitted) checked.

- SAFETY HARNESSES
  Allocated to each crew member and adjusted to fit.
  Clips checked regularly.

- FLARES
  In date - dry, handy stowage
  - crew knows where they are and how to use them.

- FIRE EXTINGUISHERS
  Well sited - serviced regularly
  - gauges show full charge.

- FIRE BLANKET
  Essential for the galley.

- LIFEBUOYS
  Securely stowed but easy to throw quickly
  - when was this last tried?

- BUOYANT LIGHT
  tested and does work.

- BILGE PUMPS
  Have been tested and do pump water out of the bilge
  and over the side. Strainers on suctions are accessible
  in case of blockage.

- FLASHLIGHTS
  Do they work?

- FIRST AID/MEDICAL KIT & MANUAL.

- WOODEN PLUGS
  One secured to each seacock.

- VHF RADIO
  Instructions posted by radio for operating,
  and for sending distress calls

- WHEEL STEERING
  Emergency tiller has been tested and crew know how to use it.

RADIO DISTRESS PROCEDURES

Fill in your call sign here ....
In fact in a distress situation the yacht's name is normally used, spelled out in the phonetic alphabet.

Phonetic alphabet

A ALPHA	**B** BRAVO	**C** CHARLIE	**D** DELTA
E ECHO	**F** FOXTROT	**G** GOLF	**H** HOTEL
I INDIA	**J** JULIET	**K** KILO	**L** LIMA
M MIKE	**N** NOVEMBER	**O** OSCAR	**P** PAPA
Q QUEBEC	**R** ROMEO	**S** SIERRA	**T** TANGO
U UNIFORM	**V** VICTOR	**W** WHISKEY	**X** X-RAY
Y YANKEE	**Z** ZULU		

Yacht's name in phonetics..

You will also need to give your own position.
* The simplest is bearing and distance *from* a known point, eg "150 degrees (True) Start Point, 5.2 miles"

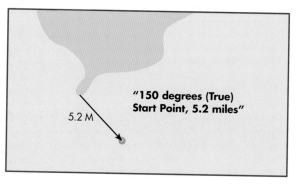

5.2 M

"150 degrees (True) Start Point, 5.2 miles"

* Alternatively, give your lat and long. Latitude comes first.

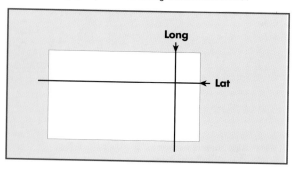

Long

← **Lat**

Even with GPS, try to give a rough indication of position ("About 10 miles south of Rocket Point") in case you get the numbers wrong.

RADIO DISTRESS PROCEDURE

MAYDAY

This distress signal is for use only when there is grave and imminent danger to a vessel or person.

- Switch to Channel 16.
- MAYDAY MAYDAY MAYDAY
- This is - yacht's name spoken three times
- MAYDAY plus yacht's name (again)
- My position is - lat and long or range and bearing from known point, or named spot.
- Nature of distress - eg 'sinking' or 'crew injured'.
- Assistance required. This is normally obvious.
- Number of people on board.
- Any other information.
- Over

PAN PAN

This is when help may be needed, but the danger *is not grave and imminent.*

- Switch to Channel 16
- PAN PAN PAN PAN PAN PAN
- Hello all stations - Hello all stations - Hello all stations
- This is - yacht's name spoken three times.
- My position is - as for MAYDAY.
- Nature of emergency.
- Assistance required.
  Over

Operating the radio in an emergency

- Train another crewman to work the radio
  - you may be needed on deck

- Paste up:
  - instructions for switching to Channel 16
  - Yacht's name spelled out phonetically
  - MAYDAY and PAN PAN procedure
  - (if GPS is carried) How to read off current position.

SECURITE (Say-cure-e-tay)

Securite - the Safety signal - repeated three times (usually by a coastal station) indicates that an important navigational or meteorological warning will follow. Eg. a severe weather warning or a buoy out of position.

GMDSS

The Global Maritime Distress and Safety System.

Was fully implemented on commercial vessels on 1 Feb 1999.
Already available to leisure craft: all are advised to have a VHF
DSC set fitted by 2005, before watch keeping on traditional VHF
channels ceases.

Yachts will require a VHF DSC set (DSC = Digital Selective Calling)
which will send the emergency call (and your position) to the
Coastguard and any ships that are nearby. Subsequent contact
will be by voice over VHF Channel 16.

Changing to DSC

- When a DSC set is installed aboard, application must be made
  for a Maritime Mobile Service Identity (MMSI) number and
  it must be programmed into the set.
- An existing Ship Radio Licence (which has to be renewed
  annually) covers DSC equipment.
- Anyone having an existing Certificate of Competence for radio
  operation must attend a short update course before operating
  a DSC radio. DSC can only be used by trained operators.
  Courses are arranged by the RYA.

Distress Procedure to be used only in the cases of
Fire/Explosion, Sinking, Flooding, Disabled and Adrift,
Collision, Abandon Ship, Grounding, Piracy/Attack,
Listing, Man Overboard.

If your VHF set is equipped with a DSC Controller:
- Lift the spring-loaded cover of the Distress Button
  and press once.
- Scroll through the Distress Menu.
  Select the appropriate distress category
  (the default setting on the menu is Undesignated).
- Lift the spring-loaded cover of the distress Button,
  press a second time
  and hold for five
  seconds to send the
  distress alert.
- Afterwards, the set will
  automatically switch to
  Channel 16. If you
  have sufficient time
  you should then send
  a traditional
  MAYDAY call by voice
  on the VHF.

Picture courtesy of
ICS Electronics, Ford

EPIRBS

Emergency Position Indicating Radio Beacons

These small, buoyant devices are another entry to the GMDSS (Global Maritime Distress and Safety System).

- When you buy an EPIRB send the card to the coastguard.
- When the EPIRB is on it transmits your position and identity. The coastguard knows where you are.
- The battery lasts approx 5 years.
- Periodically 'press to test': monthly is fine.
- Take the EPIRB into the liferaft in the panic bag. Turn it on, secure it to the cord provided and float it on the water. (There are also float-free versions.)
- The battery lasts about 48 hours in transmit mode.
- It can take up to 2 hours to communicate with a satellite and have your position fixed to within 3 miles.
- Most EPIRBS emit a homing signal which the Search and Rescue Services can use. EPIRBS also have a flashing strobe light.

- If you switch on an EPIRB by mistake leave it switched on and immediately send a Securite call to the nearest coastguard station. Tell them you have inadvertently activated your GMDSS, Reg No........................... Ask if you may switch it off. (If you had simply switched off in the first instance, they would assume you had sunk!)

If you change boats, either leave the EPIRB as is on the old one or take it with you **and re-register the serial number.** (Otherwise, the rescue services will be looking for your old boat.)

This page courtesy of McMurdo Marine.

WAYS OF CALLING FOR HELP

- Continuous sounding of fog horn.
- Rockets showing RED STARS fired one at a time or at short intervals.
- Hand held RED flares, or parachute flares.
- Smoke signal giving off ORANGE coloured smoke.
- Morse code SOS sent by any means ••• ▬▬▬ •••.
- Signal sent by radio using the spoken word MAYDAY.
- Slow and repeated raising and lowering of arms at each side.

- GMDSS.
- EPIRB transmitted signal.
- International code flags N over C.
- Signal having shape of a square over/under a sphere.
- Gun or explosive signal fired at intervals of about 1 minute.
- Flames on the foredeck (as from a burning tar barrel)!

A mobile phone is no substitute for a VHF radio - it won't work under cliffs, it can only be heard by the person you're calling and the rescue services can't DF a mobile. But if all else fails you may be able to dial 999 and ask for the Coastguard.

OTHER PROBLEMS

Keeping the Coastguard informed

- If you have a problem (eg an engine breakdown) but are not in distress, inform the coastguard on Channel 16. Keep in touch and report at once if the defect is made good. If there is a chance that help might be needed, the rescue services generally prefer to be warned in good time so assistance can be given in daylight.

Spare antenna

- In case you are dismasted carry a spare antenna that can be fitted at deck level, or a portable VHF.

Small craft safety scheme

A relative calling the Coastguard to report an overdue yacht may be unable to give a description of the vessel.

- Complete a card (CG66, available from the Coastguard, marinas & chandlers).
- The information (including full details of the yacht) is stored on the central Coastguard computer.

BAILING AND PUMPING

- Install two pumps: one operated in the cockpit and one below decks. One should be non-electric.
- Both must be operable with the hatches closed.
- Secure the pump handle to the pump with a lanyard.
- Each pump must have a strainer which is accessible.
- Carry two buckets.
- Attach a spare emergency softwood plug to each through-hull fitting.

ROPE CUTTER

- A rope or net around the propeller shaft will stop the engine, and may damage the stern gland or gearbox. Fit a rope cutter on the shaft.

ON PASSAGE

- You should report details of a major passage to the Coastguard before sailing.
- But you must inform the Coastguard on arrival (or they will waste resources looking for you).

FLARES

Red parachute rockets

Are the most effective way to raise the alarm visually.
Fire two, one after the other. Fire 15^0 downwind.

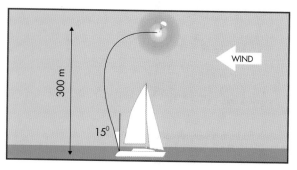

Red hand-held flares

- Can be used to raise the alarm.
- Also pin-point your position when help is on its way.

Orange smoke signals

- Used in bright conditions.

White flares

- Draw attention to a yacht. *They are not distress flares.*

If a white flare is used near the shore, inform the Coastguard in case it is mistaken for a distress flare. White flares and red flares should not be stored close together.

Make sure you and your crew know how to operate the flares. The firing mechanisms differ, but this is a common one.

- Point downwind and outboard. Pull handle base downwards.
- Twist handle until stopped, and arrow marks align
- Strike base of handle sharply with palm of hand or on hard surface. Hold by red handle only.

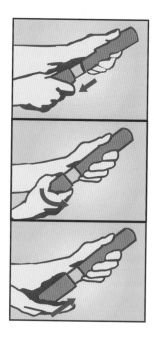

HOW MANY FLARES?

	Inshore: up to 3 miles	Coastal: up to 7 miles	Offshore: more than 7 miles	Ocean
Red hand flares	2	4	4	6
Hand held orange smoke flares	2	2		
Red parachute rockets		2	4	12
Buoyant orange smoke flares.			2	2

* Store flares in a waterproof container where they are instantly available. Flares normally last about three years. Check the expiry date each season. Out of date flares may still work and can be kept on board marked 'reserve'. Return old flares to the supplier for disposal.

LIFEJACKETS

* Carry enough for the whole crew including children's sizes (if appropriate).

Types of lifejacket

Buoyancy aid - keeps swimmer afloat but does not keep head above water. Suitable for children in harbour and dinghy sailors but not generally for use at sea.

Solid buoyancy - usually a type of PVC foam. Need no maintenance, but less comfortable for prolonged wear.

Inflatable with oral inflation Can be worn partially inflated
- Inflatable from CO_2 cylinder (manually operated)
- Inflatable from CO_2 cylinder (automatic operation).

All CO_2 inflated jackets can be topped up orally if needed.

* All inflatable lifejackets need to be tested at least once a year by inflating and ensuring that pressure is maintained for at least one hour. The CO_2 cylinders need inspection as recommended by the manufacturer.

Accessories (some may already be fitted as standard):
- reflective tape makes wearers more easily seen at night
- a whistle for attracting attention
- a light - there are various types.

Lifejackets that are combined with safety harnesses are becoming increasingly popular. In this case a crutch strap is recommended. When worn over a safety harness, some lifejackets may impede the use of the harness, although the lifejackets are still effective.
* Stow so that they are clean, dry and readily available. After issuing make sure the crew adjust the straps.

FIRE FIGHTING

A fire blanket is best for dealing with a galley fire. Do **NOT** site it over the stove, but preferably near an exit about 1.5 m above the floor.

Pull the tabs, twist so your hands are protected by the blanket and place it gently over the fire. Turn off gas/electricity and leave for 30 minutes. Throw away the blanket (or have it checked for oil impregnation).

How to use a fire extinguisher

Squirt at the BASE of the fire and employ a sweeping motion. Do not inhale.

- All purpose extinguishers are the most useful. These are the re-fillable dry powder types.
- The 1.5 kg size is good for small-to-medium sized craft.
- Have two or three; site one inside the hatch so it can be reached from the deck.
- They must be checked annually because the powder goes hard – see under Fire Extinguishers in Yellow Pages.

Action in case of fire

1 Get everyone on deck, plus the fire extinguishers.
2 Stop the boat (a breeze through the boat will fan the flames).
3 Move crew and the liferaft as far as possible from the fire.
4 Direct the extinguisher round the edge of the fire to contain it, rather than at the centre.
5 Remember also that water is an efficient extinguisher but not for liquid fires such as fat or diesel.

Automatic extinguisher for the engine compartment

Recommended for boats with engines over 25 hp.
A heat sensor automatically operates the extinguisher.

FIRST AID

The skipper or another person in the crew should have some
knowledge of first aid. One day courses are organised by the RYA.

	Kit 1	Kit 2	Kit 3
Micropore tape, 2.5 cm x 5 m	1	2	2
Non-stick dressings 10 cm x 10 cm	2	10	20
Triangular bandage, 90 cm x 127 cm	2	4	4
Wound dressings, No. 8	2	4	10
Antiseptic wipes	4	10	30
Waterproof plasters (assorted sizes)	6	20	50
Elastoplast strapping 7.5 cm rolls x 5 m	1	3	6
Scissors	1	1	1
Safety pins	4	4	4
Non-sterile examination gloves (pairs)	1	5	20
Steristrips	–	1 pack	1 pack
Tubegauz finger dressing and applicator	–	1	1
Splints	–	2	2
Eyepad	–	2	2
Anthisan cream, 30 g tube	–	1	1
Calpol (for children)	–	100 ml	100 ml
Paracetamol tablets 500 mg	–	20	100
Scopaderm TTS patches	–	4	10
Stugeron tablets, 15 mg	–	10	24
Eye drops, Predsol N 5 ml	–	–	2
Piriton tablets 4 mg	–	–	20
Non-steroidal anti-inflammatory tablets	–	–	30
Dentanurse dental kit	–	1	2

Kit 1: local sailing. **Kit 2:** coastal. **Kit 3:** offshore

In practice an additional small kit with Band Aids, seasickness pills,
etc, should be kept separately for everyday use.

To call for (free) medical advice put in a PAN PAN call.
This is addressed to the nearest coastguard.

PAN PAN MEDICO, PAN PAN MEDICO, PAN PAN MEDICO
Hello Holyhead Coastguard, Hello Holyhead Coastguard.
This is Yacht Memec, Memec, Memec
Over
HOLYHEAD COASTGUARD REPLIES:
Memec, Memec, Memec
This is Holyhead Coastguard.
Over
THEN FOLLOWS THE MESSAGE ITSELF:
Holyhead Coastguard, this is Memec. I have a medical emergency
on board. One member of the crew has been hit on the head
by the boom. He is unconscious but is breathing. He has a wound
on his forehead but has not lost much blood.

My present position is 53 degrees and 35 minutes North,
5 degrees and 8 minutes West, 25 miles from Holyhead.
I am making for Holyhead Harbour on a course 130 degrees
true at 4 knots.

HYPOTHERMIA

Hypothermia is a condition in which exposure to cold air and/or water lowers body core temperature. The symptoms include shivering, lethargy, stumbling, slurred speech, and loss of memory. The victim progressively develops a cold pale skin, slow breathing and a slow weak pulse, leading to collapse and unconsciousness.

1 Your first aim is to prevent further heat loss. Get the casualty out of the sea and out of the wind.
2 Get the casualty to the warmest spot on board and turn on all the heating. As soon as possible strip off all wet clothing, if necessary by cutting it off. Do not rub the skin to dry it, but dab it dry with a towel.
3 If the casualty is conscious get him into warm dry clothing, give him lots of warm sweet drinks and allow him to rest in a warm sheltered spot. If you have no other means of providing warmth get close enough to transfer your body heat to the casualty.
4 If the casualty is unconscious take off all his wet clothing and put him into a sleeping bag. Make sure he is in the recovery position and won't suffocate. If you have no heater, light the gas cooker.
5 If the boat will take time to warm up, get into the sleeping bag with the casualty. (Wear tight clothing to speed up transfer of heat.)

THE RECOVERY POSITION

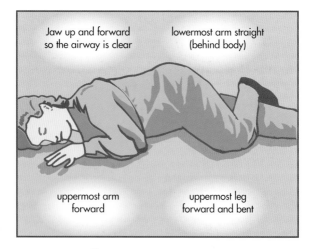

Jaw up and forward so the airway is clear

lowermost arm straight (behind body)

uppermost arm forward

uppermost leg forward and bent

The material in this section is extracted from First Aid Afloat by Dr Rob Haworth, also published by Fernhurst Books
ISBN 0 906754 88 7.

MOUTH-TO-MOUTH VENTILATION

• If you can feel and/or hear air going in and out of the casualty's mouth or nose you have no need to perform artificial ventilation. If the chest is moving violently but there is no air passing, then the airway is obstructed: open the mouth and with your finger remove any vomit, sweets or chewing gum. Remove false teeth if they are loose, but if they are firm leave them in.

1 Tilt the head back and lift the jaw upward and forward to lift the tongue clear of the airway.

• If there is no movement of air lay the casualty on his back and kneel by his right shoulder. With your right hand lift the lower jaw and push it forwards, and at the same time place your left hand on his brow and tilt the head backwards; this lifts the tongue and stops it blocking the air passage.

• Watch to see if the casualty's chest now moves rhythmically and listen for air entering and leaving. If this happens you have opened up the airway and the casualty can now breathe. If he is not fully conscious place him in the recovery position and continue to support his jaw to keep the airway open. If his chest does not move and you can sense no air movement begin artificial ventilation.

2 Pinch the nostrils together while holding the jaw up ...

• Pinch his nostrils. Keeping your right hand under the raised lower jaw place your mouth over his mouth and blow air firmly into him. You should see his chest rise and fall and you will hear the air come out again.

3 ...and, placing your mouth over his, blow firmly into him.

• After two satisfactory inflations of the chest at roughly six-second intervals check the casualty's pulse in his neck to see that there is a heartbeat. If there *is* a pulse continue artificial ventilation 12 times per minute and check the pulse every three minutes. If there is no pulse start external cardiac compression straight away. Turn to the next page.

EXTERNAL CARDIAC COMPRESSION

1 With the casualty lying flat on his back identify the breastbone (sternum). This bone runs down the centre of the front of the chest from the neck to the upper abdomen.

2 Kneel beside the casualty facing his chest and place the heel of your right hand in the centre of the casualty's chest on the lower third of the breastbone. Place your left hand on top of your right hand.

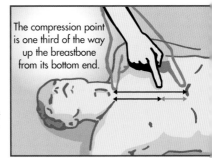

The compression point is one third of the way up the breastbone from its bottom end.

3 Rock forward with your arms locked straight and stiff so that your weight presses down on the breastbone. You will feel it move downwards with the force. The bone should move approximately 4 cm (1.5 in). Rock back so that your weight is off the casualty and the breastbone will spring upwards.

4 Repeat this cycle 100 times per minute.

5 Pause after every fifth cycle so that another First Aider can perform one cycle of mouth-to-mouth ventilation. If you are on your own, perform 15 cycles of cardiac compression, then two cycles of mouth-to-mouth.

6 Continue until you are sure that the casualty has a pulse in the neck and remains pink after you stop cardiac compression.

7 Stop mouth-to-mouth artificial ventilation only when the casualty is breathing regularly on his own.

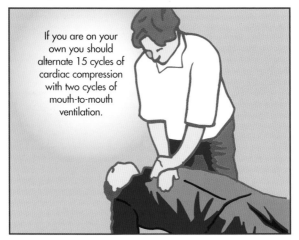

If you are on your own you should alternate 15 cycles of cardiac compression with two cycles of mouth-to-mouth ventilation.

MAN OVERBOARD (MOB)

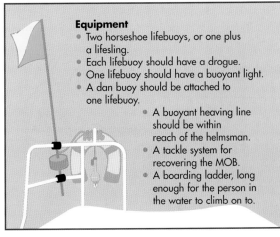

Equipment
- Two horseshoe lifebuoys, or one plus a lifesling.
- Each lifebuoy should have a drogue.
- One lifebuoy should have a buoyant light.
- A dan buoy should be attached to one lifebuoy.
- A buoyant heaving line should be within reach of the helmsman.
- A tackle system for recovering the MOB.
- A boarding ladder, long enough for the person in the water to climb on to.

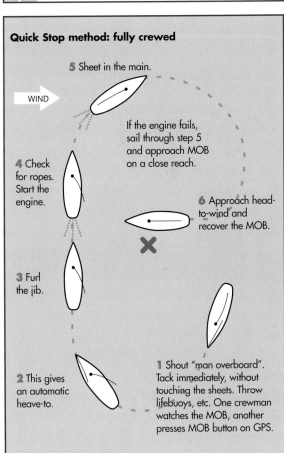

Quick Stop method: fully crewed

WIND

5 Sheet in the main.

If the engine fails, sail through step 5 and approach MOB on a close reach.

4 Check for ropes. Start the engine.

6 Approach head-to-wind and recover the MOB.

3 Furl the jib.

2 This gives an automatic heave-to.

1 Shout "man overboard". Tack immediately, without touching the sheets. Throw lifebuoys, etc. One crewman watches the MOB, another presses MOB button on GPS.

Lifesling method
This is good for shorthanded crews

1. Shout "man overboard".
2. Tack immediately.
3. Throw horseshoe lifebuoy.
4. Throw lifesling.
5. Circle the MOB (under sail or power) until the MOB reaches the line.
6. Heave to, and winch the MOB alongside.

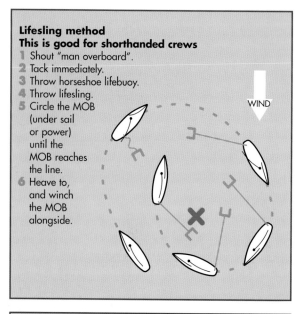

WIND

Reach-tack-reach method

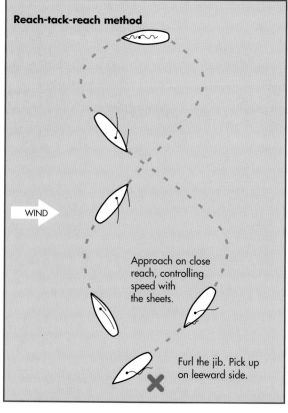

WIND

Approach on close reach, controlling speed with the sheets.

Furl the jib. Pick up on leeward side.

THE LIFERAFT

**DO NOT ABANDON
SHIP UNLESS THE BOAT
IS SINKING OR ON FIRE.**
Do not launch the raft too
early - it cannot be held
alongside for long.

1 Prepare the crew with
lifejackets, harnesses
and oilskins.
2 Prepare the grab bag.
3 Tie the raft's painter to
a strong point.
4 Check that it is tied properly.
5 Push the canister over the
lee side.
6 Give a firm tug (or tugs) on
the painter. You will hear a
bang and the raft will inflate.
7 Winch the raft alongside,
and try to jump in dry.
8 If this is impossible, clip on
to the painter and swim to
the raft.

Once aboard, adopt the
Cut Stream Close Maintain
routine:
CUT the painter
STREAM the drogue
CLOSE the door of the raft
MAINTAIN the raft and
comfort levels.

What to take

1 All rafts carry some basic
equipment. Check what is
in yours.
2 Various additional survival
packs can be packed in the
raft. These are important for
ocean sailors, less so for
coastal or short offshore
passages.
3 Whether or not raft contains
a survival pack, when offshore a grab bag for gear to
be taken aboard a liferaft is
likely to contain: portable
VHF, portable GPS, flares,
torches, leak stoppers/repair
outfit, warm clothing, water or other liquid, bailer and sponge,
simple food, first aid kit, seasick pills, insulating blanket.

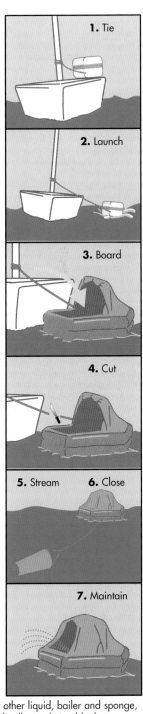

1. Tie

2. Launch

3. Board

4. Cut

5. Stream   **6.** Close

7. Maintain

TOWING

Towing in harbour
Springs, head and stern
lines plus fenders.
or
Towline though enclosed
fairlead, or bow roller
with pin in place.

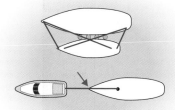

Being towed at sea
Consider one, or all, of these fixing points:

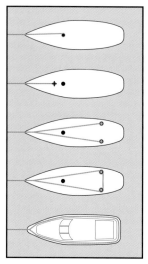

If a mast is stepped *on the
keel*, use round turn and two
half hitches around the mast,
low down.

If samson post is stepped
on keel, use that.

Otherwise, make a yoke and
take to both main winches or ...

...Take aft, around both winches
and back to itself.

For a motor yacht, take around
the superstructure.

At the bow either make a yoke or use the bow roller (with pin).

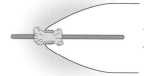

Rope packed with towels to
prevent chafe, and secured
in bow roller

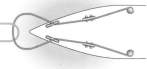

If no bow roller
make a yoke

The boat being towed must be steered. If you have lost your rudder,
stream a small drogue. At night, have someone on the VHF (or use
a portable) to communicate with the towing vessel.

Towing at sea
If one yacht has to tow another, consider doing this alongside if the
sea is calm. Rig fenders and lines as for mooring (springs, bow and
stern lines) plus others to help spread the load. Also communication
is easier when alongside. The only problems may be steering, and
slowness in slipping the tow.

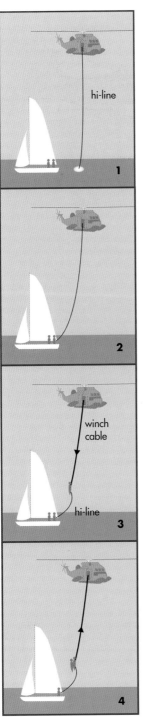

HELICOPTER RESCUE

- You will be given a channel (usually 16) to talk with the helicopter.
- The winchman will land on your port quarter. Clear the area of aerials, ensigns, etc, and the topping lift.
- You will probably be asked to motor to windward or sail close-hauled on port tack on a steady heading.

1 The helicopter will first lower a light, weighted line (the hi-line). Allow it to touch the water (to earth it).

2 Then coil the hi-line into a bucket. Do NOT tie it to the boat.

3 Use the hi-line to steady the winch cable/winch man. Haul it in as he descends.

4 Ease the hi-line as the lift is in progress. Keep enough tension to prevent swinging.

5 If a second lift is required, keep hold of the hi-line. If not, cast it clear when told to do so.

- Continue listening on Channel 16.

3 Navigation and pilotage

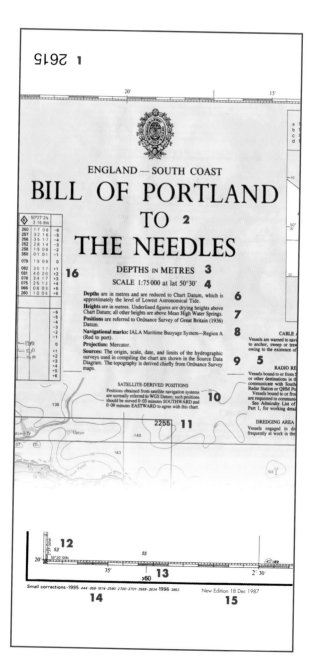

1 2615

ENGLAND — SOUTH COAST

BILL OF PORTLAND

TO **2**

THE NEEDLES

DEPTHS IN METRES **3**

SCALE 1:75 000 at lat 50°30′ **4**

16

Depths are in metres and are reduced to Chart Datum, which is approximately the level of Lowest Astronomical Tide. **6**

Heights are in metres. Underlined figures are drying heights above Chart Datum; all other heights are above Mean High Water Springs. **7**

Positions are referred to Ordnance Survey of Great Britain (1936) Datum.

Navigational marks: IALA Maritime Buoyage System—Region A (Red to port). **8**

Projection: Mercator.

Sources: The origin, scale, date, and limits of the hydrographic surveys used in compiling the chart are shown in the Source Data Diagram. The topography is derived chiefly from Ordnance Survey maps. **9**

SATELLITE-DERIVED POSITIONS
Positions obtained from satellite navigation systems are normally referred to WGS Datum; such positions should be moved 0·03 minutes SOUTHWARD and 0·09 minutes EASTWARD to agree with this chart. **10**

2255 **11**

CABLE A
Vessels are warned to navi
to anchor, sweep or traw
owing to the existence of

5
RADIO RE
Vessels bound to or from S
or other destinations in th
communicate with South
Radar Station or QHM Po
Vessels bound to or from
are requested to communica
See Admiralty List of
Part 1, for working detai

DREDGING AREA
Vessels engaged in dr
frequently at work in the

12 **13**

Small corrections·1995·444·958·1674·2590·2700·2701·3569·3834·3853·1996·3853 **14**

New Edition 18 Dec 1987 **15**

ADMIRALTY CHARTS

These are some of the details shown on an Admiralty chart.

1 **Catalogue number.**
2 **Title** - shows area covered, and used (with chart no.)
   for re-ordering.
3 **Units** used for depth measurement - normally in metres
   but watch out for older charts still in fathoms.
4 **Scale** of chart eg 1:75,000 - 1 unit of distance on chart equals
   75,000 units on earth's surface.
5 **Cautions** - printed in magenta. Contain important
   navigational warnings.
6 **Depths** are referred to Chart Datum.
7 **Underlined figures** are drying heights above Chart Datum.
   Other heights are above Mean High Water Springs.
8 **IALA buoyage system,**
   Region A - red to port when
   going into a harbour or estuary.
9 **Mercator projection** (the method
   used to construct the chart).

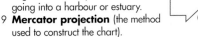

10 **Satellite derived positions.** Check your GPS programme.
11 A larger scale chart is available of this area. You should always
   be working on the largest scale chart that is available.
12 **Latitude scale.** Use this scale, opposite your position,
   for distance measurements.
13 **Longitude scale.**
14 **Small corrections** (such as buoys being moved). The year
   and number of the Notice to Mariners containing the correction.
   Admiralty charts can be corrected by returning them to a Chart
   Agent, or by yourself referring to the Small Craft Edition of the
   Notice to Mariners (four times yearly, from chart agents).
15 **Edition date.** Date this edition of chart was published.
   Chart may be latest available although published several
   years previously.
16 **Tidal stream data.** This gives tidal rate and set for hours
   before and after High Water at a Standard Port.

Charts to be carried
- A small scale chart showing the complete route (for planning).
- Detailed charts showing danger areas, eg headlands.
- Harbour plans of your departure point and destination,
  plus alternatives (in case of bad weather, etc).

Chart correction
- New editions of charts are issued from time to time, and
  charts do sometimes need correction, particularly in areas
  of shallow water where buoys may have to be moved.
  Installations such as oil rigs may also change.
- Consult the Small Craft Edition of Admiralty Notices to
  Mariners, issued quarterly and available from chart agents.

CHART SYMBOLS

Admiralty Chart 5011 is actually a book showing all the chart symbols. Here, we will just concentrate on some common dangers such as rocks and shallows. You must know these

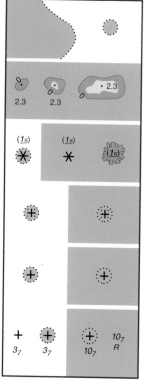

Danger line: draws attention to symbol

Rocks which do not cover, with height above high water (usually MHWS)

Rocks which cover and uncover with height above Chart Datum

Rocks awash at Chart Datum

Underwater rocks, dangerous to surface navigation. Depth unspecified

Underwater rock. Depth below Chart Datum.

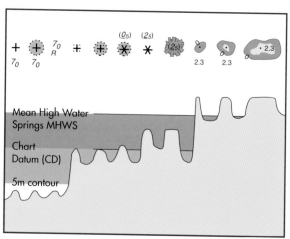

SOME OTHER CHART SYMBOLS DENOTING DANGER

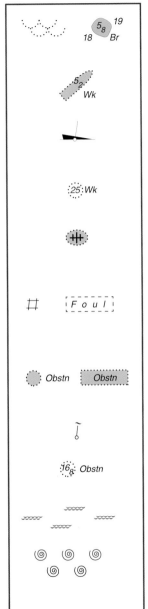

Breakers

On large-scale charts, submerged wreck, depth known

Wreck showing any part of hull or superstructure at the level of Chart Datum

Wreck over which the depth has been obtained by sounding but not by wire sweep

Wreck, depth unknown, which *is* considered dangerous to surface navigation

Remains of a wreck, or other foul area, no longer dangerous to surface navigation, but to be avoided by vessels anchoring, trawling, etc.

Obstruction or danger to navigation the exact nature of which is not specified or has not been determined, depth unknown.

Submerged pile, stake, snag, well or stump (with exact position)

Obstruction, depth known

Overfalls, tide rips, races

Eddies

PROJECTIONS

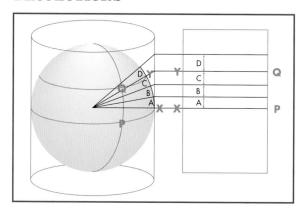

Mercator's projection

Mercator's projection is a system for projecting a globe onto a flat chart. It is the type of chart in normal use. Imagine a light at the centre of the globe, projecting each point onto a cylinder of paper. The cylinder is opened, to give the chart.

- The meridians of longitude (PQ, XY) appear parallel on the chart (in reality they converge to each pole).
- The parallels of latitude get further apart on the chart. (On the globe, distances A, B, C & D are equal - but not on the chart.)
- When measuring distances, use the latitude scale opposite your area of interest.

Gnomic projection

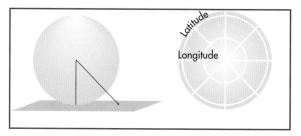

A gnomic projection is obtained by projecting from the centre of the earth onto a flat sheet, usually at one of the poles. The lines of latitude become arcs and lines of longitude are straight lines that converge at the pole. Gnomic charts are used for planning ocean passages.

A great circle is the shortest distance between two points on a globe. For a long ocean passage use a gnomic chart; the route is shown by a straight line. To sail that route you will need to make a number of course changes, eg each time you pass a meridian (angles R, S & T).

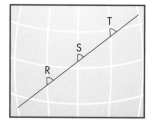

LATITUDE AND LONGITUDE

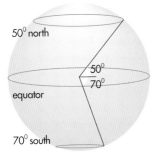

Parallels of latitude
Measured in degrees from
equator, eg 50° N or 70° S.
Up to 90°.
1 degree = 60 minutes 1° = 60'
Minutes are than divided
into tenths or hundredths,
eg 50°37'.62 N.

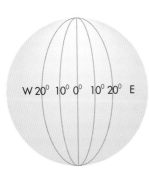

Meridians of longitude
0° goes through Greenwich
E and W measured from
there (up to 180°)
eg 10° 25'.37 E

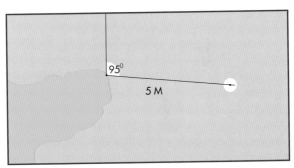

Position
Position is given as lat (first) and long, eg the position of North
Foreland Light is 51° 22'.47 N 001° 26'.80 E.
Alternatively, position can be given as a (true) bearing and
distance *from* a known point, eg, 095° North Foreland Light 5 miles.

Distance
One nautical mile = 1 minute of latitude
1M = 1' ≈ 1853 metres ≈ 2000 yards
= 10 cables ≈ 1.15 statute miles

Note: Speed is measured in knots
1 knot = 1 nautical mile per hour = 1.136 mph.

THE COMPASS

Variation

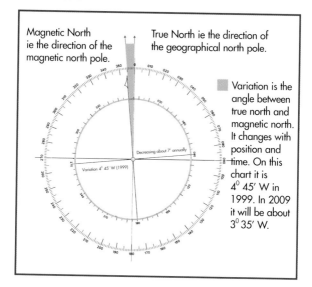

Magnetic North ie the direction of the magnetic north pole.

True North ie the direction of the geographical north pole.

Variation is the angle between true north and magnetic north. It changes with position and time. On this chart it is 4° 45′ W in 1999. In 2009 it will be about 3° 35′ W.

Decreasing about 7′ annually

Variation 4° 45′ W (1999)

Deviation

Theoretically the needle in a magnetic compass points to magnetic north, but the compass in most boats is subject to magnetic interference from the engine, the electrics and electronics. Any error caused is known as deviation.

- Deviation is the angle between a magnetic bearing and the same bearing taken by a particular compass in a particular boat.
- Unlike variation, deviation varies according to the boat's heading. To see why this is, imagine that all the 'interference' in a boat behaves as though it is concentrated into a fixed iron block.

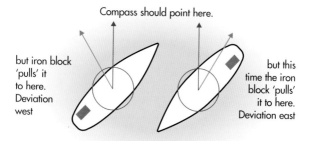

Compass should point here.

but iron block 'pulls' it to here. Deviation west

but this time the iron block 'pulls' it to here. Deviation east

In practice deviation is often reduced to a minimum or removed altogether by a compass adjuster. He will swing the compass to find out the deviation on various headings, then place magnets to remove or reduce it. He will then produce a Deviation Table for you.

A compass adjuster will produce a card like the one below showing the deviation on each heading.

As well as the actual figures, the deviation is also shown graphically. Note that the curve is symmetrical.

Swinging the compass

1 Take the handbearing compass into the dinghy, towed astern. Or stand at the backstay.
2 Sight a distant object with the handbearing compass.
3 Turn the boat through 360 degrees, taking bearings on the object. If they do not change, the handbearing compass is free of deviation.
4 Point the boat at the object. Compare the bearing from the steering compass with that from the handbearing compass. Fill in the difference as deviation on the table.
5 Repeat for various headings, and draw the curve.
6 Other methods are:

Heading	Deviation West	Deviation East
000	2	
015	1	
030	0	
045		1
060		1½
075		2
090		2½
105		3
120		3
135		3
150		3
165		2½
180		2
195		1½
210		1
225		0
240	1	
255	1½	
270	2½	
285	3	
300	3	
315	3	
330	3	
345	2½	
360	2	

a Take the boat to a known position and point at a number of distant objects whose bearings can be plotted from the chart. Compare the boat's heading with the known actual bearing.

b Point the boat along any available transits, and compare the heading with the charted bearing of the transits.

Courses and bearings

Courses and bearings are plotted on the chart in true (T).

Magnetic (M) courses are true courses corrected for variation.

The bearings taken with a handbearing compass will be (M) but deviation (if any) is applied to magnetic courses to convert them to Compass (C) - the course given to the helmsman to steer.

CONVERTING BEARINGS

1 For the order of converting types of bearing simply remember the mnemonic: <u>T</u>rue <u>V</u>irgins <u>M</u>ake <u>D</u>ull <u>C</u>ompanions.

$$\textbf{True} \xleftarrow{\;\textbf{Variation}\;} \textbf{Magnetic} \xleftarrow{\;\textbf{Deviation}\;} \textbf{Compass}$$

2 Error West, Compass Best, ie compass reads bigger.

T v **M** d **C**
$$\xleftarrow{} \; \textbf{W} = -$$

If going to the left along the row, subtract westerly deviation or variation. Add easterly deviation or variation. If going to the right, add westerly error. Subtract easterly error.

Example: Compass gives bearing 090^0. Deviation 4^0 W. Variation 3^0 W. What is True bearing?

T	v	**M**	d	**C**
083	-3	086	-4	090

Answer 083^0 T

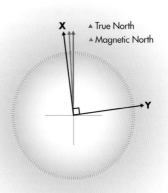

If the boat points true north, compass needle will align along X. A bearing of 090^0 Compass will be Y. From True North this is 083^0 (T)

▲ True North
▲ Magnetic North

Example: True bearing 130^0. Variation 5 degrees W. Deviation 3^0 E. What is Compass bearing?

T	v	**M**	d	**C**
W −	$\xleftarrow{}$	$\xrightarrow{}$	**W** +	
130^0(T)	+5 =135^0(M)		-3 = 132^0(C)	

Error is the sum of Variation and Deviation.

With a handbearing compass, cautiously assume deviation is zero. Check by continuously taking a bearing with the handbearing compass on a distant object, while turning the boat through 360^0.

RISE AND FALL OF THE TIDE

- In most areas there is a High Water and a Low Water every 12 hours 20 minutes.

- The size of the rise and fall varies from area to area: it might be 12 m in the Bristol Channel, 4 m off Harwich.

- **Spring tides** (springs) occur when the sun and moon are in line, relative to the earth. This happens two days after new and full moon. At springs the high tides are higher and the low tides are lower. Highest spring tides occur around 21 March and 23 September at Vernal and Autumn Equinoxes.

- **Neap tides** (neaps) occur when sun and moon are offset, midway between full and new moon. The rise and fall is smallest.

- **Range of the tide** is the difference in height between successive high and low waters.

- **Chart datum** (CD) is the level to which soundings and drying heights on a chart are referred. In practice it is the lowest height to which the tide is ever expected to fall.

- **Charted depth** is the actual sounding shown on a chart, being the depth of the sea bed below chart datum, and the least depth expected to occur in that place under normal conditions.

- **Actual depth** - at any time, is what it says, and is the charted depth plus the height of the tide, as obtained from Tide Tables.

- **Drying height** is the height above chart datum of any feature that is occasionally covered.

- **Duration** (of the tide) - the time between HW and the previous LW.

- **Mean High Water Springs** (MHWS) - the average height of all the spring highs.

- **Mean Low Water Springs** (MLWS) - the average height of all the spring lows.

- **Mean High Water Neaps** (MHWN) - the average height of all the neap highs.

- **Mean Low Water Neaps** (MLWN) - the average height of all the neap lows.

TIDE TABLES

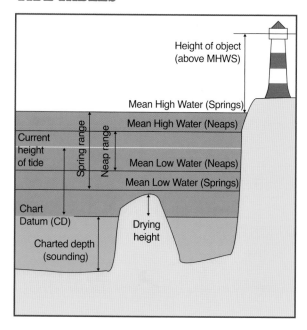

In almanacs and Admiralty tide tables, times and heights of HW and LW are given for each day for a number of large ports known as Standard Ports. Other smaller ports and harbours are listed as Secondary Ports (see p 40).

Local tide tables are available for many individual ports.

Tide tables are in this form, and are given in UT for British waters.

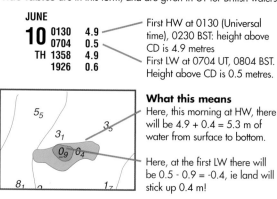

JUNE

10 0130 4.9
 0704 0.5
TH 1358 4.9
 1926 0.6

First HW at 0130 (Universal time), 0230 BST: height above CD is 4.9 metres

First LW at 0704 UT, 0804 BST. Height above CD is 0.5 metres.

What this means
Here, this morning at HW, there will be 4.9 + 0.4 = 5.3 m of water from surface to bottom.

Here, at the first LW there will be 0.5 - 0.9 = -0.4, ie land will stick up 0.4 m!

The times given in tide tables for UK ports will be in Universal Time (UT). During BST add one hour to times in the table. Tables for continental ports will show local standard time and will give a correction to adjust to UT. Boats cruising near a continental port may, of course, be using local time.

STANDARD PORTS

Tide tables give times and heights of HW and LW for a standard port. Intermediate heights and times are deduced from the accompanying curve.

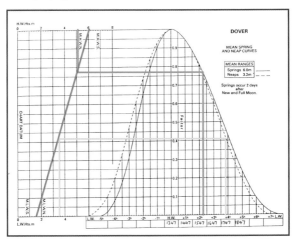

FEBRUARY

	Time	m
16	0136	6.4
	0852	1.1
M	1347	6.1
	2100	1.2

Range is 5.3.
Nearer springs

Required: the height of tide at Dover at 1557.
1 On the Dover tidal diagram plot heights of HW and LW each side of the required time and join them up with a sloping line (red).
2 Enter the HW time and other times as necessary in the boxes below the curves.
3 From the required time 1557 draw a line vertically to the curve (green). The range on the day concerned is nearer the Spring range and therefore the Spring curve (solid line) is used.
4 Proceed horizontally to the red sloping line and hence vertically to the height scale to read 5.1 m.

Required: the time at which the afternoon height of the tide falls to 3.5 m.
1 Plot in the times of HW and LW and join them with a sloping line (red) as before.
2 Enter HW time and others to cover the required event.
3 From the required height (3.5 m) proceed vertically (yellow) to the sloping line (red) and then across to the spring curve. Dropping down to the time scale, required time is 1737.

SECONDARY PORTS

For each Secondary Port there are a set of corrections (known as 'differences') to be applied to the figures for the relative Standard Port. For example: Penzance

Standard Port DEVONPORT (→)							
Times				**Height (metres)**			
High Water		Low Water		MHWS	MHWN	MLWN	MLWS
0000	0600	0000	0600	5·5	4·4	2·2	0·8
1200	1800	1200	1800				
Differences PENZANCE							
−0055	−0115	−0035	−0035	+0·1	0·0	−0·2	0·0

It helps to remember that the left hand side deals with the time differences and the right side with heights - two separate issues. Note this table is in Universal Time.

These corrections are irregular. For instance, in the example above, if the time of HW Devonport is around 0000 or 1200, the correction to be applied for Penzance is -55 min. But if the Devonport HW is around 0600 or 1800, then the correction is -75 min (1 hr 15 min). In this particular case there is no variation in the differences for LW.

Similarly, when the height of HW Devonport is 5.5 m, HW at Penzance will be 0.1 m higher. When the height at Devonport is 4.4 m, HW at Penzance will be no higher.

Clearly there are times when interpolation is needed. For instance in the figures above there is a 20 minute difference between the corrections for a 1200 HW and an 1800 HW. So, interpolating 'by eye' the correction for a HW around 1500 would be -65 minutes.

Interpolation can be carried out graphically as the following two examples show.

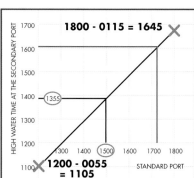

What is the time of HW Penzance when HW Devonport is 1500 UT?

Ans HW Penzance is 1355 UT

Remember: work in UT and convert to BST at the end, if necessary.

When LW Devonport is 2.0 m what is LW Penzance?

Ans 1.86 m ≈ 1.9 m

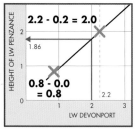

SECONDARY PORTS –
intermediate times and heights

The procedure for calculating the height of the tide at secondary ports at intermediate times between HW and LW is essentially the same as for standard ports. There are no tidal curves for secondary ports, so the curve for the appropriate standard port is used. We 'pretend' this is the curve for the secondary port, and put onto it the secondary port's times and heights.

What is the height of tide at 1300 BST at Penzance?

Use the example of Penzance on the previous page when the tide table for Devonport shows:

7		
	0348	4.7
	0955	1.4
TU	1614	4.9
	2221	1.4

HW Devonport = 1614 UT = 1714 BST
From table on previous page HW Penzance = 1604 BST (green line).

Use the Devonport curve as a 'pretend' Penzance curve, and mark in this time of HW.
HW Devonport = 4.9
and interpolating **HW Penzance** is 4.9 (4.9-0.0)
LW Devonport is 1.4
and interpolating **LW Penzance** is 1.3 (1.4-0.1)
Add these to the 'Penzance' curve.
Read off the height of tide at 1300 as previously:

Answer 3.6 m.

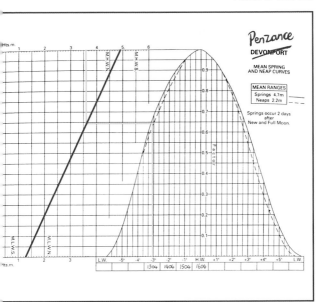

LOCAL TIDES

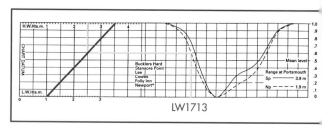

LW1713

For some areas there is a stand at high water, or two high waters.
The curve is based on the more predictable LW, then used as before.

The 'Rule of twelve'

This gives a useful approximation of intermediate heights, although
it should not be used where the tide is irregular.

Assuming about six hours between high and low water, this rule says
that the rise and fall of the tide is:

1/12 of range in 1st hour	2/12 of range in 2nd hour
3/12 of range in 3rd hour	3/12 of range in 4th hour
2/12 of range in 5th hour	1/12 of range in 6th hour
(1,2,3 - 3,2,1)	

**Example: tidal range is 4.4 m at Port X. How much
will the tide have fallen 2 hours after HW?**

Tide will have fallen 1/12 + 2/12 of the range = 1.1 metres

Thus far we have been looking at the height of tide.
Now let's look at the flow of water.

TIDAL STREAMS - DEFINITIONS

Tidal streams are the horizontal movement of the water caused
by the vertical rise and fall. If the tide drops in a harbour, then
the water has to flow somewhere! The stream normally changes
direction about every six hours, although the change is not
necessarily at local HW or LW.

Set (expressed in three figures - eg 160 degrees) is the direction
in which a tidal stream flows measured in degrees True.
Note: The wind's direction is FROM where it blows. A tidal set
indicates the direction the stream flows TOWARDS.
Rate (in knots) is the speed at which a tidal stream flows.
Drift is the distance the stream carries in a period of time.
A tide race occurs where a strong tidal stream passes through
a narrow passage, or off a headland. Dangerous, especially if
wind against tide.
Overfalls are caused by tide flowing strongly over an
uneven seabed.

TIDAL STREAM INFORMATION

Tidal stream charts

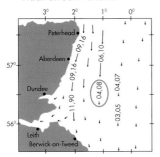

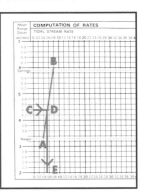

- Very useful for passage planning
- Come in sets of 12 (Almanacs or Tidal Stream Atlases)
- Arrows indicate direction of stream (degrees T)
- Length and thickness of arrow indicates strength
- Rate indicated by figures, eg 04,08 means 0.4 knots neaps, 0.8 knots springs
- Comma indicates position data was recorded
- Interpolate if between springs and neaps

7
0359	1.5
0918	5.9
1627	1.5
2135	6.0

Example: What is the tidal stream off Dundee? Range is 4.4 m. Draw AB on the Computation of Rates table. From 4.4 draw CD. DE gives the interpolation, 0.5 knots.

The information from tidal diamonds is more detailed than the atlases, but may be very localised.

- Very useful for course to steer and course made good.
- Position of ◇ will be shown on the chart. Lat and Long are also given.

Take 2 hrs before HW Dover as an example. From 2.5 hrs to 1.5 hours before HW the stream runs at 218° T. At springs it runs at 1.0 knots, at neaps 0.5 knots. Interpolate between springs/neaps, depending on range at Portsmouth (see green lines opposite). Tidal stream is 0.9 knots.

10
0627	1.0	range
1121	6.5	5.5
F 1848	1.0	
2337	6.5	

Tidal Streams referred to HW at DOVER

Hours	◇ Geographical Position	◇ 49°34'ON 6 40 OW		
	Directions of streams (degrees)	Rate at spring tides (knots)	Rate at neap tides (knots)	
Before High Water 6	-6	078	0·7	0·4
5	-5	113	0·6	0·3
4	-4	160	0·8	0·4
3	-3	203	0·7	0·4
2	-2	218	1·0	0·5
1	-1	237	1·2	0·6
High Water	0	251	0·8	0·4
After High Water 1	+1	283	0·4	0·2
2	+2	343	0·6	0·3
3	+3	019	0·8	0·6
4	+4	033	1·0	0·5
5	+5	044	0·9	0·5
6	+6	055	0·7	0·4

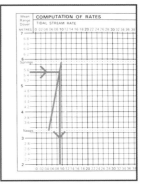

HOW TO OBTAIN TIDAL SET (DIRECTION) AND DRIFT (DISTANCE) OVER A PERIOD

Example. Find the set and drift near ⬦A from 1100 to 12.30 on 23 August.

- Find the nearest tidal diamond (in this case ⬦A) or tide arrow.

- Look up the relevant tide tables (Dover, in this case)

23 **0603** 1.0
1054 6.5
TH **1821** 0.9
2318 6.5

Tidal Streams referred to HW at DOVER				49°34'ON 6 40 OW	
Hours	⬦ Geographical Position			⬦	
Before High Water 6 5 4 3 2 1	Directions of streams (degrees)	Rate at spring tides (knots)	Rate at neap tides (knots)	-6 078	0·7 0·4
				-5 113	0·6 0·3
				-4 160	0·8 0·4
				-3 203	0·7 0·4
				-2 218	1·0 0·5
				-1 237	1·2 0·6
High Water				0 251	0·8 0·4
After High Water 1 2 3 4 5 6				+1 283	0·4 0·2
				+2 343	0·6 0·3
				+3 019	0·8 0·6
				+4 033	1·0 0·5
				+5 044	0·9 0·5
				+6 055	0·7 0·4

HW Today = 1054 UT + 1 hr
= 1154 BST
Range Dover = 5.5 m

- Make a Tidal Set and Drift Table (below). Enter time of HW (11.54). Tide is given for half an hour before to half an hour after this (11.24 to 1224). Mark up rest of times.
- Our period includes half an hour at the HW-1 rate, and one hour at the HW rate.
- Interpolate between Springs and Neaps.

So the tidal effect in $1\frac{1}{2}$ hours is:

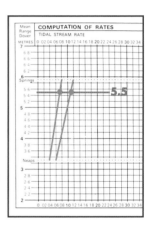

COMPUTATION OF RATES — TIDAL STREAM RATE (Mean Range Dover). 5.5

TIDAL SET and DRIFT TABLE

	TIME	⬦	SET	RATES			DURN.	DIS
				SPRINGS	NEAPS	INTERPLN		
BEFORE H.W.	-6 -5 -4 -3 -2							
	-1 ⟩1024	A	237°T	1.2	0.6	1.1	½	0
IGH WATER	1154 ⟩1124 1224	A	251°T	0.8	0.4	0.7	1 hr.	0
	+1							
AFTER H.W.	+2 +3 +4 +5 +6							

1. Insert HIGH WATER times
2. Add/subtract 30 mins to give start and end of HW tide.
3. Complete TIME column.

4. Insert appropriate DIAMOND, SET and RATE.
5. Interpolate RATES if necessary.
6. Compute duration of RATE if less than one hour.
7. Calculate length of drift (rate × duration).

BASIC CHARTWORK

Dead Reckoning (DR) is plotting a position based on the course steered and distance travelled in a given time.

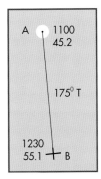

Position at 1100 was A.
Log reads 45.2
Course of 175° T was steered until 1230 when log reading was 55.1.
Hence a distance of 9.9 M has been travelled in the direction 175° T and the DR position at 1230 is B.

Dead reckoning makes no allowance for the effects of wind or tide, and thus may be only a theoretical position. But it is still an important part of basic navigation, and far better than having no plot.

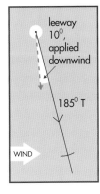

Leeway is the sideways effect of the wind on a boat under sail.
The boat is pushed sideways down-wind so that its water track is different from the course actually steered.

The effect of leeway depends on varying factors including hull design. It will be felt most when a boat is going to windward and heeled over, less with a beam wind and nil with the wind astern. Leeway is also affected by wind strength and boat-speed and is greatest at slow speed in strong winds.

Leeway can be assessed by looking aft and estimating the difference between the wake and the fore and aft line. But in strong winds, when leeway is likely to be greatest, the sea may be rough and the wake hard to see.

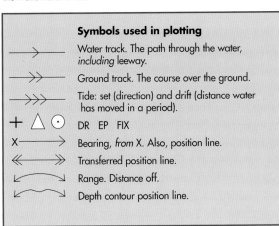

Symbols used in plotting

Water track. The path through the water, *including* leeway.

Ground track. The course over the ground.

Tide: set (direction) and drift (distance water has moved in a period).

DR EP FIX

Bearing, *from* X. Also, position line.

Transferred position line.

Range. Distance off.

Depth contour position line.

ESTIMATED POSITION

An EP is a DR position with compensation for leeway and the tidal stream. Obtain the tidal set and drift from the tidal atlas (rough) or from tidal diamonds (for accuracy).

Example:

From the DR already obtained, find the EP. Assume the tidal set and drift are as calculated on page 44,

ie 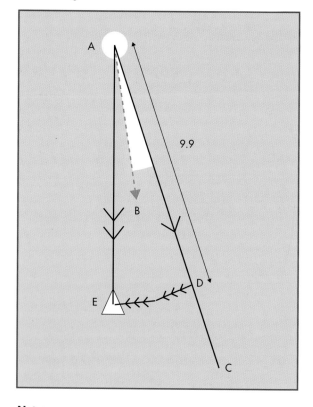 during the 1.5 hr period.

1 'Dot' your course line AB.
2 Apply leeway and draw the water track AC.
3 Measure off the distance run AD.
4 Apply the tidal effect from D, to give the EP at E.
5 Draw the ground track AE.

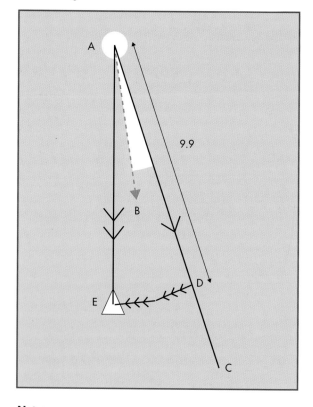

Note:
* When plotting an EP, apply leeway first.

Note:
* You actually move along the line AE.
* You have travelled (over the ground) AE in 1.5 hrs so your speed over the ground (SOG) is AE/1.5.

COURSE TO STEER: ALLOWING FOR THE TIDE

Clearly it is better to plot a course that compensates for the wind and tide and lets you 'make good' your required course.

Example
Starting from point A at 1100 it is required to make good a course of 175^0 to reach point B. Boatspeed is estimated at 5 knots, and tidal stream is as for the previous example. Westerly wind, leeway 10^0.

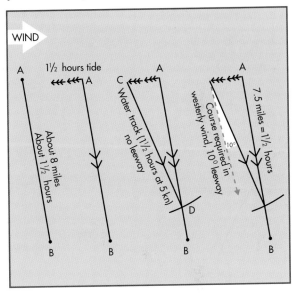

1 Draw Ground Track between start point and target (AB). Measure the distance approximately.
2 Anticipate average achievable speed and determine likely passage time (5 knots, about 1.5 hours).
3 Extract, interpolate and construct the tidal vectors (set and drift).
4 From C arc off the distance vector (average speed x anticipated time). This meets AB at D.
5 Join up this arc mark to the end of tide vector - this is the WATER TRACK CD.
6 Length along Ground Track to the arc mark is the Distance Made Good (AD).
7 Calculate Speed Made Good by dividing this by anticipated time (see Point 2): AD/1.5.
8 Work out ETA from $\dfrac{\text{Dist to go}}{\text{Speed Made Good}}$ + start time
9 Add or subtract leeway to "oppose" the tide.
10 Convert Water Track from degrees (T) to degrees (C) to give Course to Steer.

Note: Plotting a Course to Steer, apply leeway at the end.

POSITION LINES, TRANSITS, DEPTH CONTOURS

Taking bearings

Anything that can be seen, and positively identified on the chart, can be used for taking a bearing. It need not be a man-made object; isolated rocks and the edges of bold headlands are fine. It is best to identify the objects, then write them in a notebook. Then the times can be written alongside. As it is easy to take three bearings within a minute, one time does for all. But take the abeam bearings last.

Position lines and fixes

A single bearing of an object is a position line. It is of limited value on its own but can often be combined with other information. A fix is obtained by using two or more position lines.

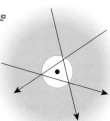

Transits

Aligning two conspicuous objects gives a very accurate position line.

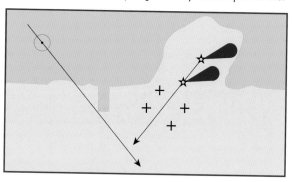

Depth

A steeply shelving sea bed gives a good indication of position, after you have 'reduced to soundings' by subtracting the height of tide from the echo sounder reading.

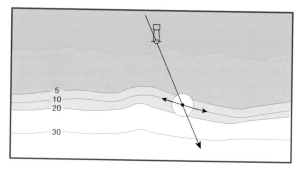

Fixes

Objects too close together   This is better
increase chance of error

Three bearings can produce the most
accurate result. Angles of cut from 30⁰
to 150⁰ apart are ideal.

Cocked hats

Most three-point fixes will end in a 'cocked hat'.

Usually take the   If near a danger,   Try another one!
point in   take the point
the centre.   nearest the danger.

RISING AND DIPPING DISTANCE

light just breaks the surface

TABLE 3(4)	Lights – distance off when rising or dipping (M)									
Height of light					Height of eye					
metres	feet	metres	1	2	3	4	5	6	7	8	9	10
metres	feet	feet	3	7	10	13	16	20	23	26	30	33
10	33		9.7	9.4	10.2	10.8	11.3	11.7	12.1	12.5	12.8	13.2
12	39		9.3	10.0	10.8	11.4	11.9	12.3	12.7	13.1	13.4	13.8
14	46		9.9	10.7	11.4	12.0	12.5	12.9	13.3	13.7	14.0	14.4
16	53		10.4	11.2	11.9	12.5	13.0	13.4	13.8	14.2	14.5	14.9
18	59		10.9	11.7	12.4	13.0	13.5	13.9	14.3	14.7	15.0	15.4

Example

• Height of light on chart is
11 m above MHWS. Look
up MHWS, eg 2 metres.
Work out current height of
tide, eg 1.1 m. So add 0.9
(2-1.1) to height of light.
11 + 0.9 = 11.9 m. This
gives actual height of light
above the surface. Height of
eye estimated to be 2 m.

So distance off = 10.1 nautical
miles (from table)

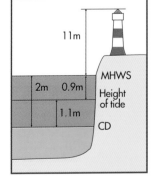

RUNNING FIX

If only one object is available, a fix is still possible by using the log.

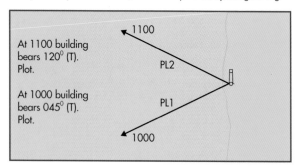

At 1100 building bears 120° (T). Plot.

At 1000 building bears 045° (T). Plot.

PL2

PL1

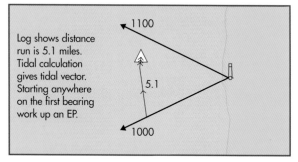

Log shows distance run is 5.1 miles. Tidal calculation gives tidal vector. Starting anywhere on the first bearing work up an EP.

5.1

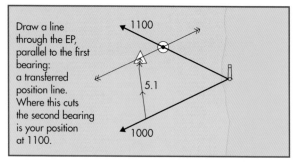

Draw a line through the EP, parallel to the first bearing: a transferred position line. Where this cuts the second bearing is your position at 1100.

5.1

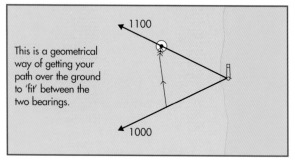

This is a geometrical way of getting your path over the ground to 'fit' between the two bearings.

IDENTIFYING LIGHTS

All lights used as navigational aids have individual characteristics.
These are shown alongside the light on the chart,
eg Berry Head Fl(2) 15s 58m 14M.
The characteristics are shown in this order:
(a) Rhythm - the distinctive periods of light and dark,
eg Fl, Oc, etc (see below).
(b) Colour - if no colour is shown a light is assumed to be white.
(c) Period - how quickly the rhythm is repeated. Eg Fl(2) 15s
means the cycle of two (white) flashes plus a period of darkness
is repeated every 15 seconds.
(d) Elevation - the height in metres of the light above MHWS
eg 58 metres.
(e) Range - the distance in (nm) that the light can be seen
in normal visibility, eg 14 M.

Colours

Major long range lights are always white, because that colour can
be seen the furthest. Apart from white, red and green are the most
common colours for lights. Yellow lights are used only on Special
Marks. Other colours such as blue or orange are very unusual.

Light characteristics

These are the principal types, there are some variations.

FIXED - steady light   F
(easily confused with a shore
light and not much used).

FLASHING - period of light   Fl
is shorter than period of dark.

GROUP-FLASHING
- eg Fl(2). Older form is GpFl(2).   **Fl(2)**

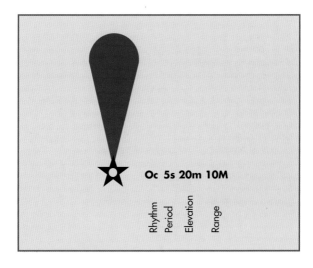

Oc 5s 20m 10M

Rhythm Period Elevation Range

OCCULTING - the period of light is greater than the period of dark. Older form is Occ.   **Oc**

GROUP-OCCULTING - eg Oc(3). Older form is GpOcc(3)   **Oc(3)**

ISOPHASE - equal periods of light and dark.   **Iso**

QUICK - repetition rate 50 to 79 (usually 50 or 60) flashes per min.   **Q**

VERY QUICK - repetition rate 80 - 159 (usually 100 or 120) flashes per min. Older form VQFl.   **VQ**

LIGHTS SHOWING MORE THAN ONE COLOUR

Alternating lights (eg Al WR) show different colours in succession. This type of light is rare in Europe.

Sectored lights When a multi-coloured light is not shown as an alternating light (ie 'Al' is not in the characteristic) then it will be a sectored light. Eg Fl WR 30s 15m 12-10M. This is a light, flashing every 30 seconds, showing a white light in some sectors and red in others. Note

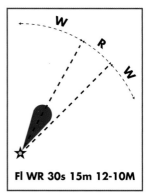

Fl WR 30s 15m 12-10M

that two ranges are given, as the range of the red light will be shorter than the white light.

Sectored lights can either be used to warn of a danger or to show the safe line of approach to a port.

Note: When a sectored light is described in a light list or almanac, the bearings of the sectors are given from seaward.

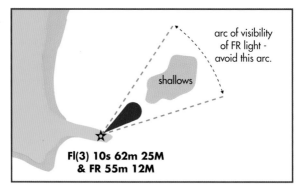

arc of visibility of FR light - avoid this arc.

shallows

Fl(3) 10s 62m 25M & FR 55m 12M

ELEVATION AND RANGE OF LIGHTS

The elevation of a light (it is easier to talk about its height) is the height of the light above MHWS, and is given on a chart in metres (m).

The actual range at which a vessel will see a light depends on the height of the light, its power, the height of eye of the observer, and the atmospheric conditions at the time. There are several ways of expressing range, but on charts and in almanacs it is shown as **nominal range** - the luminous range when the meteorological visibility is ten nautical miles. This takes no account of the earth's curvature. So the actual range at which a light is sighted on any occasion will not be exactly as shown on the chart.

The range at which a light is first seen or at which it dips below the horizon can be a useful way of obtaining a position: see page 49.

The **loom** of a major light - the glow in the sky - can under clear conditions often be seen when the light is still below the horizon and beyond its nominal range.

BUOYS AND BEACONS

Used in inshore waters to warn of dangers to navigation, mark the limits of navigable channels and the approaches to channels. Also to mark certain other features.

A buoy's function is indicated by its **shape, colour, top-mark,** and (where lit) the **characteristic** of its light.

SHAPES
- conical, can, spherical, pillar, or spar.

COLOURS
- normally green (G), red (R), black (B), yellow (Y), white (W), or a combination of these; and are indicated by a letter under the buoy.

(Note: This letter shows the colour of the buoy, not of the light - although it may be the same.)

TOPMARKS - Cones (or pairs of cones), spheres, cans. A radar reflector may also be shown. If buoys are lit, this chart symbol  is shown on the chart.

In shallow water a beacon may be used in place of a buoy In this case the shape of its topmark indicates the type of buoy it is replacing. So the term **marker** may refer either to a buoy or a beacon.

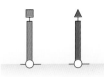

IALA BUOYAGE

The system of buoyage, including standard shapes, colours etc, and used throughout Europe is known as the IALA system, (International Association of Lighthouse Authorities).

DIRECTION OF BUOYAGE - a starboard hand buoy marks the starboard side of the channel when entering harbour. This direction is usually obvious, but where any doubt may exist, this symbol shows the direction of buoyage.

IALA System A

Lateral marks

Port hand.
Light:
red, any rhythm.

Starboard hand.
Light:
green, any rhythm.

Modified Lateral Mark
You **could** go either side, but one is preferred.
  Preferred channel to starboard   Preferred channel to port

Isolated Danger Mark
Light: White Fl(2)
Isolated danger with
clear water all round.

Safe Water Mark
Light: Isophase or occulting
or 1 long flash every 10 seconds
or Morse 'A'(**- —**). Usually placed
at the approach to a channel
- shows safe water all round.

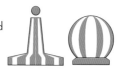

Special Mark
Not a navigational mark but indicating a special feature.
Light (when fitted): Yellow. Any characteristic that does not conflict
with nav. marks. May be any shape, topmark (if any): Yellow X.

IALA SYSTEM B

Lateral buoys in the USA

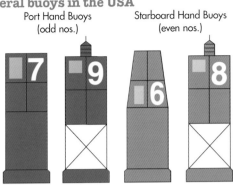

Port Hand Buoys
(odd nos.)

Starboard Hand Buoys
(even nos.)

In the USA the buoyage system for entering harbour
is different from most other places.

Cardinal marks

Cardinal buoys indicate the direction in which a particular danger
lies, and the side on which it is safe to pass.

- A north cardinal lies to the north of the danger, and the clear
  water is on the north of the buoy.
- The characteristics of the light refer to the figures on a clock
  face. (LFl = long flash.)

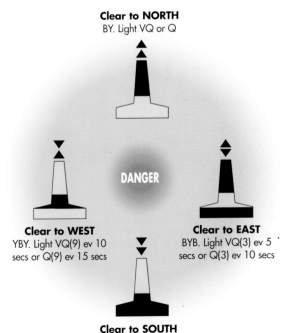

Clear to NORTH
BY. Light VQ or Q

DANGER

Clear to WEST
YBY. Light VQ(9) ev 10
secs or Q(9) ev 15 secs

Clear to EAST
BYB. Light VQ(3) ev 5
secs or Q(3) ev 10 secs

Clear to SOUTH
YB. Light VQ(6) + LFl ev 10 secs or Q(6) + LFl ev 15 secs

FOG SIGNALS

Are sounded from lighthouses, light vessels and buoys. There are various types - the abbreviation (in brackets) is how they are shown on the chart.

DIAPHONE (Dia) - operated by compressed air, gives a powerful low pitched sound that often ends in a grunt.

FOG HORN (Horn) - uses compressed air or electricity to operate a diaphragm. Some produce sounds of a different pitch.

REED (Reed) - operated by compressed air, varies but generally higher than diaphone or horn.

EXPLOSIVE (Explos) - sounds like a gun. Now not often found.

Fog signals on buoys: **Bell (Bell), Gong (Gong), Whistle (Whis).** These may be mechanical or operated by wave action. Operation by wave action is clearly irregular. If a precise characteristic is given eg Horn (1) 15s then operation must be mechanical.

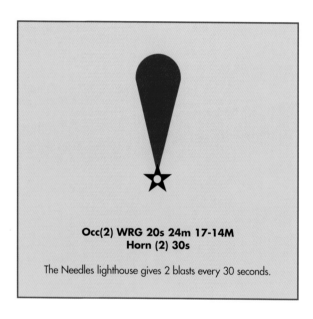

**Occ(2) WRG 20s 24m 17-14M
Horn (2) 30s**

The Needles lighthouse gives 2 blasts every 30 seconds.

PASSAGE PLANNING

General passage planning checklist.
- Charts: overall passage, headlands, harbours?
- Weather forecast. NB fog, etc - avoid heavy traffic and areas where pilotage is difficult.
- Traffic separation schemes: avoid if possible, join at end or at an oblique angle. Cross at right angles.
- What time is HW? Springs/neaps?
- How do we ensure maximum tidal advantage?
- Ring on the chart any dangers.
- What are the alternative harbours/anchorages (ie bolt-holes)?
- Can we get in after dark if we're late?

Preliminary chartwork

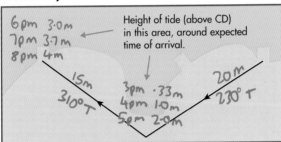

6 pm 3·0 m
7 pm 3·7 m
8 pm 4 m

Height of tide (above CD) in this area, around expected time of arrival.

15 m   20 m
310°T   3 pm ·33 m   230°T
               4 pm 10 m
               5 pm 2·0 m

- Plot the planned route, with courses and distances (check again when passage starts).
- What is the distance? How long will it take?
- How will the tide affect timing?
- What is the tidal height at any crucial shallow areas for various times of arrival?
- Are there any tidal gates - areas such as the entrance to harbour, narrow channels or exposed headlands where the tidal stream runs strongly? Should departure time be adjusted to avoid the worst of a foul tide or catch a favourable one?
- What navigation aids are there (lights, buoys, conspicuous features)?
- How far off should headlands be passed? Usually well off unless pilot recommends inshore passage. Are there tide races or overfalls?

Harbours
- Have we got the right chart?
- Does the pilot book/almanac cover the harbour?
- Is the entrance well marked or easily recognised and can it be entered safely without local knowledge?
- Are there any unmarked dangers?
- Is the approach and entrance well lit and is entry possible at night?
- Is entry possible at any state of the tide?
- Is there a bar or off-lying shallow water that might be dangerous? Therefore is the entrance safe in all weathers?
- Once inside, is there sufficient depth to lie at all states of the tide?
  So, overall, is this harbour a possibility?

PILOTAGE

Pilotage is the process of navigating by using visible geographical features, marks and buoys. You will use the chart, compass, echosounder and radar to follow a predetermined track to your objective.

- Work out the height of tide. The actual depth = height of tide + charted depth. This immediately gives a clue to where you are. Know whether the tide is rising or falling and what the tidal streams are doing.
- When identifying an object, always take a bearing on it. Check this with the expected bearing from the chart, to make sure it's the one you're after.

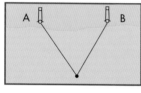

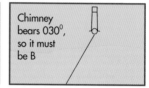

Chimney bears 030°, so it must be B

Buoy hopping

The most common form of pilotage.
Identify each buoy as you pass it. If you miss buoy B, and go straight from A to C, you will hit the putty.
If the buoys are far apart, plot a course from buoy to buoy.

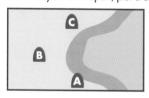

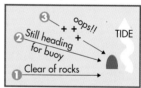

Heading straight for a buoy in a cross-tide can lead to danger.
Steer a compass course to the buoy, or watch the GPS Cross Track.

Using bearings

You could use a bearing on the church to enter the bay, but a small error will put you on the rocks. Similarly, a back bearing on the church will help you out of the bay (355°).

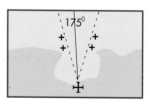

Transit/leading lights

Much better to have a transit (the church and windmill) or leading lights. Any natural or man-made objects that line up can be used.
Note: Bearings on the chart are True bearings from seaward (eg 270°).

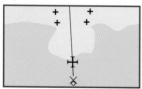

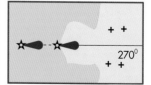

CLEARING BEARINGS

As you enter the harbour the church should bear not less than 005° (or you'll hit A) and not more than 030° (or you'll hit B). You can even tack in, between these bearings. Convert to °C for the helmsman.

A clearing transit is even better. Keep the flagstaff 'to the left' of the church.

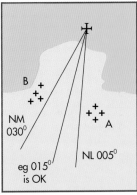

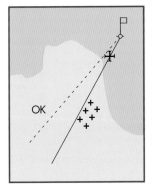

To miss the rocks keep A and B in transit until C and D come into line, turn to starboard and keep C and D in transit.

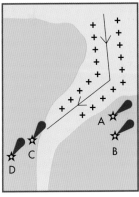

Single transferred position lines

This can be used to give the initial lead through a channel or into a harbour. The safe bearing into the harbour is plotted on the chart and a parallel line drawn through a previous conspic. object. The log and time are plotted when the vessel picks up this first bearing and then you run the distance (over the ground) between the two bearings before turning on the bearing into the harbour.

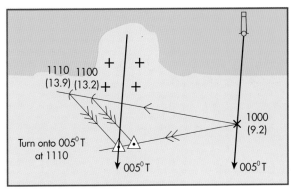

PILOTAGE PLAN

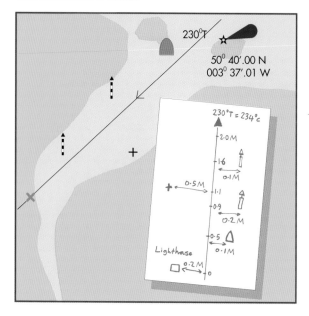

It is useful to summarise the objects you will pass, the expected log reading as you pass and their distance off your planned track.

Can we enter the harbour safely in the present conditions?

* If in doubt, stay out. A shallow harbour entrance with a strong onshore wind, or a rock-strewn entrance in fog, is bad news.
* Approach from a known position - eg a buoy or a GPS fix.
* Taking bearings from this fixed position can help identify features on the shore and the lights on navigation marks against the background of shore lights.

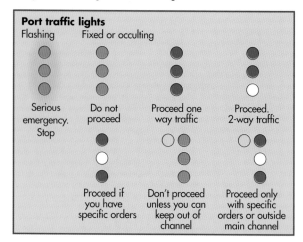

Port traffic lights

Flashing	Fixed or occulting		
Serious emergency. Stop	Do not proceed	Proceed one way traffic	Proceed. 2-way traffic
Proceed if you have specific orders	Don't proceed unless you can keep out of channel	Proceed only with specific orders or outside main channel	

NIGHT SAILING

Navigation offshore can often be easier at night because lights can be identified positively at a distance. After a night passage, an arrival shortly after dawn is often good because lights seen well offshore help establish a position and then entry into harbour can be made in daylight.

Inshore at night lit buoys in a well-marked and lit channel - for instance in the approach to a commercial port - can be hard to distinguish from shore lights in the background. The solution is careful planning.

1. Do not take any short cuts at night, even if there is plenty of water. Stay in the buoyed channel (or close outside if there is heavy commercial traffic - and if there is enough water).
2. Plot the course from lit buoy to lit buoy, and measure the distances. Then you will always know where the next buoy lies and can look out for it - 'We're passing No.4 buoy now. No2 buoy bears 350°, that's fine on the port bow, it's just under half a mile and shows a red light flashing to every ten seconds'.
3. Start from a certain position, eg close to a buoy. Then carefully identify each buoy as you pass it so that you always know where you are.
   If a harbour with a complex approach channel seems daunting, plan an entry in daylight.

SAILING IN FOG

There are two hazards for small craft sailing in fog - being run down by a larger vessel (or colliding with another small craft), and going aground. The bigger hazard is being run down. For this reason the safest place is in shallow water, preferably at anchor.

If fog is forecast:
1. Get clear of any heavy traffic areas.
2. When inshore, plan a course that keeps clear of hazards that will be dangerous in poor visibility.

If fog is detected:
1. Take a fix and plot an EP.
2. Hoist the radar reflector.
3. Increase lookout - and listen. Ears are better than eyes. Slow the engine, or stop, to listen.
4. If radar is fitted - keep radar watch.
5. Put on lifejackets (in case you are run down).
6. Make a sound signal at two minute intervals
   – ·· (sail) or – (power)
7. Keep white flares to hand.
8. Slow down.
9. Use GPS.
10. If plotting a course from buoy to buoy, beware of boats doing the same thing!

Tactics in fog:
1. Attempt to make harbour (see panel below).
2. If can't a) Sail out of shipping lane and heave to, *or*
   b) Sail to shallow water and anchor.

For reaching harbour in fog:
Method 1 - Running a contour

This works well in medium or steeply shelving water, with no
rocks. Otherwise don't try it.

1 Work out the height of the tide and hence the depth of water
   at your chosen contour. Is the tide rising or falling?
2 Aim off (so you will later know which way to turn) and head
   in towards the shore.
3 When the echosounder gives your required depth,
   turn towards your destination.
4 *Zigzag* your way along the contour, until you find the
   fairway buoy.

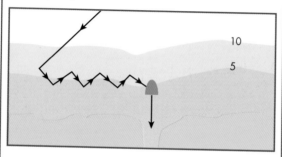

Method 2 - Buoy hopping in fog

This works well if the buoys are not too far apart and if there
is no danger 'behind' the buoy if you miss it. You must have
a contigency plan in case you miss the buoy - if you haven't
don't buoy hop.

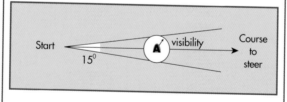

Will you find buoy A? Draw a circle around it, whose radius
is the visibility. From your starting point draw a cone, angle 15^0
(you can steer to about 7^0) You should find buoy A.
Will you find buoy B? This is further away, and the 15
degree cone may mean you miss it.

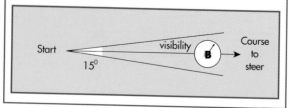

We are grateful to that expert navigator Tom Cunliffe for the ideas behind this panel.

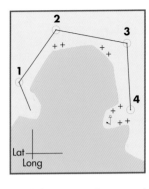

GPS

Waypoint navigation
* A waypoint is a point you want to pass through on the way to your destination. A set of these defines the passage - make sure the route between them avoids all dangers.
* Record the lat. and long. of Waypoint 1 and enter in the GPS, not forgetting North/South and East/West eg 50^0 41'.37 N 002^0 30'.29 W
* Label it WP1, and note it in the log.
* Repeat for WP2, WP3, WP4.
* When you set out, the GPS will give a range and bearing (in degrees True or Magnetic - your choice) to WP1.
* Convert to degrees Compass and set off for WP1.
* Use the cross-track function to check your progress. This records your position when the function is switched on and 'draws' a line from it to WP1. It then shows your distance off the direct line. eg At A we are 0.6 miles off course, and should turn left.

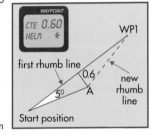

* Suppose you drift off course (to A), the quickest route from A to WP1 is to plot A, work out the new course to steer but increase the offset (to port). Start the cross track again. This time you should sail straight down the rhumb line, fine-tuning the offset so you do. (This assumes there are no hazards on the new course. Otherwise, turn hard left and go back to the original rhumb line.)

Finding your position
* Use the GPS to give your lat. and long. at regular intervals. Plot this fix on the chart, with the time, in case the GPS goes down.
* You can do this more quickly by entering a convenient way-point (one you have no intention of visiting). Then ask the GPS its range and bearing, and work back to your present position. The compass rose makes a very good waypoint for this purpose, as you have the (True) bearing immediately.

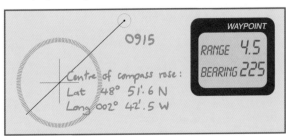

Course Over the Ground (COG) and Speed Over the Ground (SOG)

The GPS gives your COG (True or Magnetic - your choice) and SOG. Comparing this with the compass and speedo gives a measure of the tide and leeway.

Man overboard function

Press the MOB button. The GPS enters this as a waypoint and will give you the lat. and long. and the range and bearing back to the position. Note that the victim will drift away from this position.

Using GPS on a long passage (where there is more than one tide)

1 Work out the overall tidal effect. In this case the first 12 hours cancel out.

2 This gives a course to steer. You may need to allow for leeway, also.

3 Put in your final destination as the target waypoint, unless there is a hazard en route.

4 During the first 12 hours use GPS and EP to plot your position every 2 hours. Adjust your course if necessary so you arrive at A – the required position uptide of the waypoint.

5 In the last 15 miles use GPS to check your Bearing to WP and see if it changes. If the bearing is steadily drifting, turn slightly until it stabilises.

6 Alternatively, start the GPS again from A and steer so the cross track remains constant But don't yaw wildly back-and-forth to keep it to zero. Remember, a one degree change of course gives one mile deviation in a 60 mile trip.

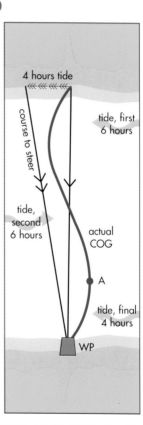

4 hours tide

tide, first 6 hours

course to steer

tide, second 6 hours

actual COG

A

tide, final 4 hours

WP

1° ——————————— 1 mile

←———————————→
60 miles

7 As soon as you have identified your destination, get a transit and keep that constant.

KEEPING A LOG

TIME BST	COURSE ORDERED (°C)	LOG READING	ESTIMATED COURSE STEERED	ESTIMATED DIST RUN	ESTIMATED LEEWAY	WIND	SEA	WEATHER	Vis	Bar	POSITION	SOURCE OF FIX	NEXT WP
											DATE FRIDAY 27 July FROM Denhaven to L'Aberpêche		
0700	⊥	–	–	–	–	NW3	Calm	0/8	G	15	Denhaven Hr	Vis	–
0800	Var	–	Var	–	–	"	"	"	"	"	" entrance	Vis	1
0900	250	2.7	250	2.7	3°	"	slight	"	"	15½	Griddle Pier	Vis	4
1000	"	6.5	"	3.8	"	NW4	mod	"	"	"	54°11.2 N : 01°13.4 E	RN	"
1100	"	10.9	"	4.3	4°	"	"	"	"	"	54°10.1 N : 01°10.5 E	"	"
1200	185	15.8	190	4.7	NIL	"	"	"	"	16	54°06.2 N : 01°09.4 E	"	29
1300	"	20.6	"	4.7	"	"	"	"	"	"	54°01.1 N : 01°08.7 E	"	"
1400	"	25.6	"	4.9	"	"	"	3/8 H	"	"	53°55.0 N : 01°07.3 E	"	"
1500	"	29.7	185	4.1	5°	WS	"	"	"	17	53°52.2 N : 01°05.2 E	"	"

REMARKS
HW Dover 0856   LW 1603   **5**
0740 start engine 0750 Slip under power. Co + Sp to clear Hr – WP1 Dep Fix 0805 WP1. a/c 240. Set full main + Gen. Sp 3kts. Set Log 0 Stop engine 0830 Bench Bn ← 1'. L 1.2   0855 Griddle Pier ↦ ½ L 2.5 a/c 250   **6** 0915 Wind inc. Furl gen 0925 T.S. now fair
1115 WP4 a/c 185 L 12.0. unfurl gen   **7**
1230 Fix NN
1520 WP 29 a/c 160 L 31.5   **8**

It should be possible to plot a vessel's position at any time from the information in the log. Use a new page for each day.

1 Work in BST.
2 Work in degrees Compass and convert for chartwork.
3 Log gives distance run.
4 Estimate course steered.
5 HW and LW at relevant port.
6 Note landmarks and record them.
7 Record sail changes (affect leeway)
8 Record changes of course: especially when tacking.
9 Watch for changes in barometric pressure - reassess plan if more than 3.5 mb change in 3 hours (rising/falling quickly).

From *Logbook for Cruising under Sail* by John Mellor/Fernhurst.

4 The Rule of the Road

GENERAL

The formal title is The International Regulations for Preventing Collisions at Sea, also known as the Colregs. Here they will be called the Rules.

The Rules cover: Steering and Sailing Rules (who gives way to whom), Lights and Shapes, and Sound and Light Signals. In addition Distress Signals are dealt with in an appendix to the Rules (but on page 14 of this book). The Rules are lengthy and complex because they have to cover every eventuality at sea. Here we are dealing only with those Rules that are of importance to small craft.

Definitions (Rule 3)
Underway means not attached to the ground.
Making way means moving through the water
Power-driven vessel includes a sailing vessel motor sailing or, of course, motoring.

Lookout (Rule 5)
Every vessel shall maintain a proper look-out (by sight, hearing, etc). This is the most important rule.

Risk of Collision (Rule 7)
If there is any uncertainty about the risk of collision with an approaching vessel, then take a series of compass (not relative) bearings with a handbearing compass.
If the other vessel is large, take bearings of her stern. If those compass bearings do not change appreciably, then there must be a risk of collision. Take action according to Rules 11-18.

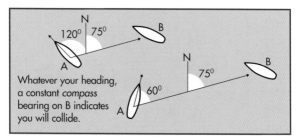

Whatever your heading, a constant *compass* bearing on B indicates you will collide.

Action to avoid collision (Rule 8)
- When two vessels are close it is essential that each vessel understands what the other is doing.
- Any alteration of course to avoid collision must be bold, so that it is clear that course has been altered. Just missing a bigger ship is neither clever or good seamanship. Take positive action in ample time and with regard to good seamanship.
- Avoid a series of small alterations of course. This is important at night when the change in aspect of her navigation lights is the only indication that a vessel has altered course.

Narrow channels (Rule 9)

There is no formal definition of a narrow channel, but any large vessel is likely to consider that the buoyed approach channel to a harbour or port is a narrow channel and expect small craft to keep clear.

- Vessels navigating in narrow channels and fairways must keep to starboard.
- Small craft under 20 m and sailing vessels must keep clear of larger vessels that can only navigate in the channel. And they must not pass ahead of such a vessel.
- Do not anchor in a narrow channel or fairway.

Traffic separation schemes (Rule 10)

These are established in areas where there is heavy shipping traffic and they are shown on all charts.

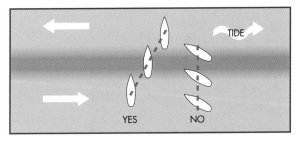

- Small craft should, if possible, use the Inshore Traffic Zones.
- If small craft have to use a traffic lane they must follow the correct direction for the lane and they must not impede larger vessels.
- If it is necessary to cross a traffic lane, make sure your heading is at right angles to the lane, cross as rapidly as possible and keep clear of vessels that are using the lane.
- Don't anchor in or near a traffic separation scheme.

THE BASIC STEERING AND SAILING RULES FOR VESSELS IN SIGHT OF ONE ANOTHER.

Both vessels under sail

When each has the wind on a different side:
Port tack gives way, Starboard has right of way (Rule 12)

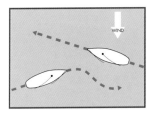

When both vessels have the wind on the same side:
Windward vessel gives way (Rule 12).

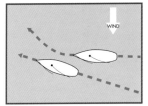

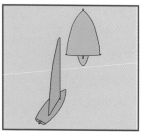
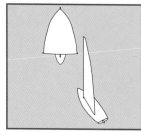

When you are on port tack and are in doubt about port/starboard, keep clear.
Red can't tell if green is on port or starboard, so assumes starboard and keeps clear.

When on starboard tack, it is likely that an approaching vessel under spinnaker is to windward of you - so stand on, taking care in case you have not been seen.

OVERTAKING

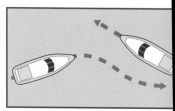

An overtaking vessel (power or sail) must keep clear of the vessel being overtaken. But the vessel being overtaken must not hamper the overtaking vessel (Rule 13)

Vessels under power

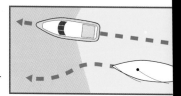

Head-on situation
Power vessels approaching head-on should alter course to starboard, passing down each other's port side (Rule 14). 'Green to green, red to red, perfect safety go ahead.'

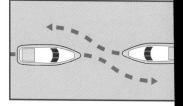

Crossing situation
If two power vessels are crossing, the vessel with the other on her starboard side should keep clear (Rule 15). 'If to starboard red appear, 'tis your duty to keep clear.'

Remember: Take early and substantial action (Rule 16).

Stand-on obligation (Rule 17)
a) If in right, maintain course and speed.
b) May take evasive action if give-way vessel does not.
c) Do not turn to port with the vessel on port side.
d) This does not absolve give-way vessel's obligation.

RESPONSIBILITIES BETWEEN VESSELS (RULE 18)

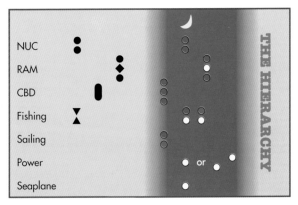

NUC
RAM
CBD
Fishing
Sailing
Power
Seaplane

THE HIERARCHY

A vessel must give way to any vessel above it in the list, except in narrow channels, traffic separation schemes and when overtaking. In other words:

A vessel under power gives way to:
- a vessel not under command (NUC)
- a vessel restricted in ability to manoeuvre (RAM)
- a vessel engaged in fishing
- a sailing vessel (but see below).

A sailing vessel must keep clear of:
- a vessel not under command (NUC)
- a vessel restricted in ability to manoeuvre (RAM)
- a vessel constrained by draft (CBD)
- a vessel engaged in fishing.

Small craft - large ships

The Rules may say that, with the exceptions shown above, power gives way to sail. But in practice this increasingly applies only to power boats and small commercial vessels.
- Large commercial vessels cannot stop or alter course quickly. A laden tanker may travel several miles after she has stopped her engines.
- Commercial vessels are now often travelling fast. The time between another ship being a comfortable distance away, and being dangerously close, can be unexpectedly short.
- Small craft can be hard to see from the bridge of a large vessel, especially when the bridge is aft.

Generally small craft should keep clear of large commercial vessels both in confined water and in the open sea - but always making it clear beyond doubt that they are getting out of the way.

Restricted visibility (Rule 19)
a) Proceed at safe speed adapted to visibility.
b) When using radar, also maintain listening watch.
c) Keep clear of shipping lanes and channels.

LIGHTS AND SHAPES

The lights shown by various vessels fit into two categories:

a) Navigation lights. These are the lights that any vessel must show from sunset to sunrise and also in restricted visibility. They vary according to a vessel's size and there are different lights for vessels under power and under sail.

b) Distinguishing lights (and shapes). In addition to showing navigation lights, vessels employed in certain activities (eg towing or fishing) or in certain situations (eg not under command) also show distinguishing lights by night and shapes by day. For this reason it is logical to list shapes and distinguishing lights together.

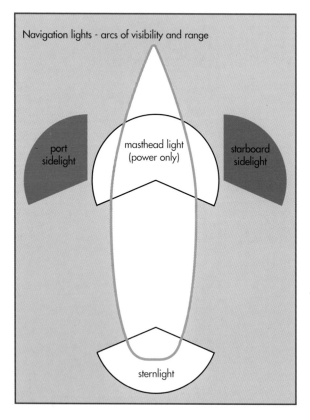

Navigation lights - arcs of visibility and range

port sidelight

masthead light (power only)

starboard sidelight

sternlight

Required ranges for vessels up to 20 m (65 ft)

YACHT SIZE	7m - 12m	12m - 20m
Tricolour lantern	2 miles	2 miles
Masthead light	2 miles	3 miles
Side lights	1 mile	2 miles
Stern light	2 miles	2 miles

POWER-DRIVEN VESSELS UNDERWAY (RULE 23)

| Stern | Port side | Bow |

Over 50 m

Masthead light – second masthead light aft and higher – sidelights – sternlight.

Under 50 m

 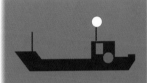

Masthead light – sidelights and sternlight.

Under 12 m

May show all-round white light (instead of masthead light and sternlight) + sidelights.

Under 7 m & speed under 7 knots

May show all-round white light only.

VESSELS UNDER SAIL (RULE 25)

Stern	Port side	Bow

Sidelights & sternlight only – no masthead light

Under 20m may have combined masthead lantern
(red/green/white) with no other lights.

(Rare) A yacht may carry an all-round red over green,
plus side and stern lights

A sailing yacht when motor sailing shows the same lights
as a power vessel. So engine on, masthead lights on.

By day: Sailing vessels using
their engines for propulsion but
with sails hoisted should show
forward a cone, point down.

VESSELS AT ANCHOR (RULE 30)

Under 50 m   **Over 50 m**

All round white   A second white light aft   By day:
light forward.   (lower than for'd light).   one ball.

Note: *Yachts over 7 m must display an anchor light.*
Under 7 m need not, unless near a fairway or anchorage.

VESSELS AGROUND

Stern   Port side   Bow

Under 50 m: two all round red lights plus anchor light.

 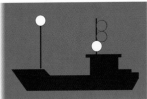 

Over 50 m: two all round red lights, plus anchor lights

Three vertical balls.

Note: vessels under 12 m need not exhibit
lights or shapes when aground.

TOWING (RULE 24)

The tow is measured from the stern of the tug to the stern of the tow.

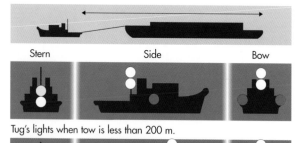

Stern   Side   Bow

Tug's lights when tow is less than 200 m.

Tug's lights when tow is more than 200 m.

If the tug is more than 50 m it will also carry a second (white) masthead light aft of, and higher than, the forward one.

Vessel being towed.

By day: Diamonds only needed if tow exceeds 200 m.

VESSELS NOT UNDER COMMAND (RULE 27)

(eg with mechanical or steering breakdown)

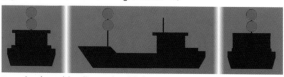

Two clearly visible all round red lights.
Note: although it is unlikely that a vessel not under command would be using her engines, she would, if making way, show navigation lights as well as NUC lights.

By day:
two balls.

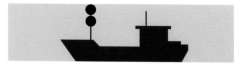

VESSELS RESTRICTED IN THEIR ABILITY TO MANOEUVRE (RULE 27)
(eg dredgers, tugs)

Stern   Port side   Bow

Three all-round vertical lights: red/white/red, plus sidelights etc. if making way).

By day, three vertical shapes: ball/diamond/ball.

A working **dredger** shows two vertical red lights on obstructed side and two vertical green lights on clear side - as well as Restricted in Ability to Manoeuvre lights (and navigation lights if making way).

By day: two vertical balls on obstr- ucted (working) side, and two diamonds on side where it is clear to pass, in addition to restricted in ability to manoeuvre shapes.

Diving tender
Flag 'A' or rigid replica.
Although diving tenders rarely operate at night, when doing so they must show the vertical red/white/red lights indicating restricted in ability to manoeuvre.

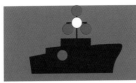 

Mine clearance vessels exhibit three all round green lights or balls, plus lights for power vessel or lights/shapes for anchored vessel. Do not approach this vessel within 1000 m.

Vessel constrained by draught (Rule 28)

Stern   Side   Bow

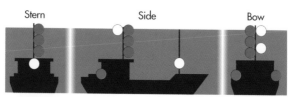

Vessel constrained by draught (eg a vessel confined to the centre of a channel) shows three vertical all-round red lights as well as normal navigation lights.

By day a vertical cylinder.

Fishing vessels (Rule 26)

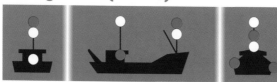

Vessel trawling (ie towing some kind of net):
All-round green over white lights. Show regular navigation lights when making way, but not when stopped.

Vessel fishing (other than trawling)

All-round red over white lights, plus sidelights and sternlight (if making way). When outlying gear extends more than 150 m an all-round white light (or, by day, a cone - point up) in the direction of the gear.

By day: trawlers and fishing vessels show a shape consisting of two cones with their points together.

Pilot vessel (Rule 29)

By day

SOUND SIGNALS

Vessels in sight of each other

One short blast
I am altering my
course to starboard.

Two short blasts
I am altering my
course to port.

Three short blasts
My engines are
running astern.

Five (or more) blasts
Your intentions are not
understood. Keep clear

Vessels in a narrow channel in sight of each other

**Two long & one
short blasts**
I intend to overtake you
on your starboard side.

**Two long & two
short blasts**
I intend to overtake you
on your port side.

Morse Code 'C'
I agree to be overtaken.

One long blast
I am approaching
a bend in the channel.

Note: one long blast, in reply, by an approaching vessel.

Vessels in restricted visibility

One long blast
every 2 minutes
Power vessel underway.

Two long blasts
every 2 minutes
Power vessel stopped.

One long & 2 short blasts
every 2 minutes
Vessels under sail.
Also: vessels fishing,
towing, NUC, RAM, CBD.

Morse Code 'B'
every 2 minutes
Vessel under tow (if manned).

Vessels at Anchor

Rapid ringing of bell
for 5 seconds every minute.

**Vessel over 100m
at anchor**
Bell rung forward.
Then gong rung rapidly
aft for 5 seconds.

May sound morse Code 'R' ■ ▬ ■ to warn approaching vessel.

Vessels aground

Three rings of bell   Anchor signal   Three rings of bell

5 The weather

THE WEATHER

There are four weather rules for skippers:
- Know how to get forecasts, both before sailing and when at sea.
- Always get a forecast before going to sea. Clearly this helps planning and is essential in marginal conditions and with a less strong crew. (A recent survey showed that 18% of regular sea-goers hardly ever, or never, checked the weather forecast before sailing.)
- At sea, listen to forecasts regularly and keep a 'weather eye' open for local changes. Enter barometer readings and weather conditions in the log.
  The less settled the weather, the more important this becomes.
- Know enough about weather to understand forecasts fully, and recognise what you see on a weather map.

GETTING FORECASTS

The Met Office publishes an excellent free booklet - 'Marine Weather Services' which gives information on all sources of marine forecasts. Copies are available from the Met Office or by calling 08700 750 075 or Fax 08700 750 076.
Note: times, frequencies and telephone numbers below may change.
Television. TV weather maps will not give detailed local information, but their excellent graphics give a very clear and useful picture of the overall situation. Worth looking at the night before sailing.
BBC Shipping forecast. Radio 4 (198 kHz or 94.4 m).
0048, 0535, 1201*, 1754*. *LW only.
Also www.met-office.gov.uk
Inshore forecast. Radio 4 0048, 0535.
Local Radio. Many BBC Local Radio Stations broadcast coastal weather information, mostly during summer months only.
Details of times and frequencies are found in local newspapers and in almanacs and in RYA booklet G5.
Marinecall. Charged at 60p/min. Recorded Met Office forecasts up-dated at least twice daily. 09068 500 + local area number. These can include 3-5 day forecasts for advance planning. (Help desk is 0171 729 8811.)
Metcall Direct. This service, payable by credit card, allows direct consultation with a forecaster, and can be useful when the best possible information is important (eg, in planning a return passage across the Channel) 08700 767 888.
Metfax. This fax service can provide a range of information by fax. These include 2-day inshore forecasts and 2-5 day area planners and charts which are fine for planning passages. To call up the service there are different numbers for the areas required; these numbers are shown in the Met Office booklet or from Metfax Helpline 08700 750 075.
The excellent weather map and the clarity of the information make this a valuable service.

Coastguard. Channels 10 and/or 73 VHF (after an announcement on Ch.16). Area forecasts every 4 hours. Strong Wind Warnings (Force 6 or more) broadcast as received and every 2 hours.

Navtex. This requires Navtex equipment on board. Produces printed weather information, including gale warnings, as well as navigational and other information.

Weather Centre. Telephone.
www.met-office.gov.uk changing to www.metoffice.com

BBC Shipping forecasts (for times see above).

* Some of these may be at inconvenient times (although it is possible to record them automatically) but because they cover all NW Europe, they help to provide a valuable overall picture of the weather, and are a useful back-up to local forecasts. They can also be used to draw a simple weather map on board (see page 86).

There are four elements in a Shipping Forecast:
a) Gale warnings (if any) (b) General synopsis (c) Area Forecasts (d) Coastal station reports (not at present included in 1201 and 1754 forecasts). Certain specific forecast terms must be understood:

Gale warning:
Imminent =   within 6 hours of time of issue
Soon =   within 6 - 12 hours of time of issue
Later =   within 12 - 24 hours of time of issue
A gale indicates winds of Force 8 (34 - 40 knots) or gusts of 43 - 51 knots within the area, but may not be over whole area. Severe gale indicates winds of at least Force 9 (41 - 47 knots) or gusts reaching 52 - 60 knots.

General synopsis
Systems movement:
Slowly =   moving at less than 15 knots
Steadily =   15 - 25 knots
Rather quickly =   25 - 35 knots
Rapidly =   35 - 45 knots
Very rapidly =   more than 45 knots

Area forecast
Visibility (in nautical miles):
Very good =   more than 30 miles
Good =   5 - 30 miles
Moderate =   2 - 5 miles
Poor =   1000 m - 2 miles
Fog =   less than 1000 m

Coast Station Reports
Note that mean pressure is 1013 mb.
Barometric pressure change/tendency in last 3 hours:
Steady =   movement less than 0.1 mb
Rising or falling slowly =   change of 0.1 - 1.5 mb
Rising or falling =   change of 1.6 - 3.5 mb
Rising or falling quickly =   change of 3.6 - 6.0 mb)
Rising or falling very rapidly = more than 6.0 mb
Now rising or falling =   change from rising to falling
                                (or vice versa) in the last three hours.

Beaufort Wind Scale

Force	Knots	Metres/sec	Description	Sea state
1	1 - 3	0.5 - 1.5	Light breeze	Smooth
2	4 - 6	2 - 3	Light breeze	Calm
3	7 - 10	3.5 - 5	Gentle breeze	Few white horses
4	11 - 16	5.5 - 8	Mod breeze	Small waves
5	17 - 21	9 - 10.5	Fresh breeze	Larger waves
6	22 - 27	11 - 13.5	Srong breeze	Rough
7	28 - 33	14 - 16.5	Near gale	Very rough
8	34 - 40	17 - 20.5	Gale	High seas
9	41 - 47	21 - 24	Strong gale	Severe seas
10	48 - 55	24.5 - 28	Storm	Very severe conditions

WEATHER MAPS

Weather maps to be seen in the UK generally cover most of NW
Europe and the Atlantic approaches.

While it is essential to get regular local forecasts, a weather map
allows a broader view. It helps understand the features behind
a local forecast, and gives a better idea how the weather may
change. Weather maps can be received on board with a Navtex,
Metcall or radio fax, but can be obtained before sailing from the
Metfax system. They can also be compiled on board from BBC
shipping forecasts, as described below.

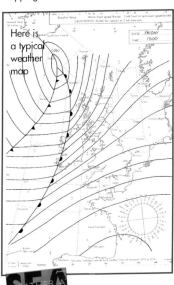

Here is a typical weather map

Weather terms

There is no room here
for a detailed study
of what causes the
weather (meteorology
is its full title), but it is
essential to understand
the features referred to
in weather forecasts and
seen on weather maps.

Note:
A veer is when the
wind shifts clockwise.

A back is when the
wind shifts anticlockwise.

A full discussion is given in the Fernhurst book
Weather at Sea by David Houghton: ISBN
1 898660 49 2.

Isobars. Lines joining places with the same barometric pressure, similar to contours on a land map. Isobars close together indicate strong winds.

Depressions or 'lows'. Areas of low pressure.
- In the Northern hemisphere the wind blows anticlockwise round depressions, not exactly parallel to the isobars but at an angle of approx. ten degrees towards the centre of the low (ie backed).
- Low pressure areas and their associated fronts (see below) are generally areas of unsettled weather with strong winds and rain. They can move quickly, and in NW Europe their movement is usually (but not always) easterly or north easterly. The forecast movement of a low cannot be precise (eg 'moving slowly north east and expected to be in German Bight by 0600 tomorrow') and frequently it may change direction or speed.

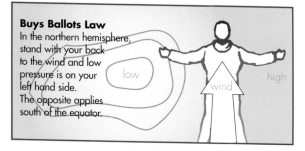

Buys Ballots Law
In the northern hemisphere, stand with your back to the wind and low pressure is on your left hand side. The opposite applies south of the equator.

low

wind

high

Troughs (of low pressure). These may be compared to valleys on a regular map. The weather in a trough is generally the same as in the associated low.

Anticyclones or 'highs'. The wind blows clockwise round an anticyclone or high. These are fair weather systems, and well spaced isobars indicate generally light winds. Movement is often slow.

Ridges (of high pressure). May be compared to mountain ridges and have fine weather as in an anticyclone.

Air masses.
These do not appear on weather maps, but they are the main cause of fronts which *do* appear. Air masses are large volumes of air of mostly uniform character. Those affecting NW Europe are named according to where they come from (arctic, polar, tropical), and whether they

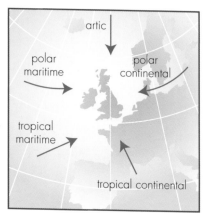

artic

polar
maritime

polar
continental

tropical
maritime

tropical continental

originate from over the sea (maritime), or from over a continent (continental). Hence 'polar maritime', 'tropical continental' etc.

Fronts. A front is the boundary between two kinds of air. A warm front is caused when a mass of warmed air overtakes and rises over a mass of cold air. Similarly a cold front is created when a mass of cold air pushes in under warm air. A front may sometimes be described in a forecast as a trough.

An occlusion occurs when a cold front catches up with a warm front. The cold air pushes in under the warm air. The weather is often similar to a warm front.

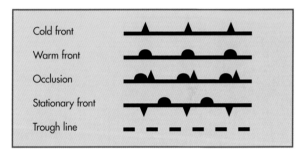

Cold front

Warm front

Occlusion

Stationary front

Trough line

Clouds

Cirrus = feathery	Cumulus = heap	Cirro = high
Alto = mid-height	Nimbus = raining	Stratus = layer

Level	Name	Description
High level 11,000 m	Cirrus	Mares tails
	Cirrocumulus	Mackerel-like sky
	Cirrostratus	Halo around sun
Mid level 5,000 m	Altocumulus	Mackerel sky
	Altostratus	Featureless layer
	Nimbostratus	Raining
Low level 2,000 m	Stratocumulus	Rolls
	Stratus	Featureless
Across all levels	Cumulonimbus	Rain/thunder
	Cumulus	Cotton wool

Lows and their associated fronts are the type of weather system that can most affect our weather. They normally herald bad (or less settled) weather and this is what sailors need to know about.

If the weather pattern around a low is understood, its position on a weather map, or in a forecast, will give an important indication of the wind in the area, and plotting its predicted movement, even if approximate, will show likely future weather.

PASSAGE OF A DEPRESSION

Observer is stationary in open water;
the depression is moving quickly NE.

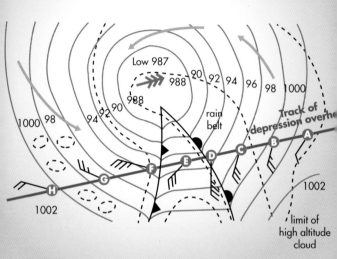

	H	G	F	E	D	C	B	A	Pos'n
Time	23.30	19.00	14.00	11.30	09.45	07.10	04.00	01.00	
Wind	WxN4	NW5	WxN7/8	SW6	S7/8	SSW6	SxW5	SW2	
Baro	1001 ↑	997 ↑	993 →	993 —	993 ↓	996 ↓	999 ↓	1001 —	
Cloud	None	Large Cumulus	Cumulo Nimbus	Stratus	Cloud	Lowering	Thickening	Cirrus & Cirro Stratus	
Weather	Fair	Showers	Rain/ Showers	Drizzle	Rain in last hr.	Continuous Mod. rain	Fair	Fair	
Sea State	Swell from NW	Mod. NW	Rough W/SW/NW	Mod. SW	Rough S&SW	Mod. SSW	Mod. SSW	Slight SW swell	
Visibility	Good	Good	Poor	Mod. to Poor	Deterio- rates	Deterio- rates	Good	Good	

Courtesy of the RYA.

SEA BREEZE

A *sea breeze* blows from seaward towards the land and can
be a significant feature along the coast in summer. It is caused
by warm air rising over the land and air moving in from the sea
to take its place. The sea breeze normally develops in the morning
with a clear sky or light cloud, and by afternoon it may reach
Force 4 or 5. It dies at sunset. As the day passes, the direction
of a sea breeze will veer (in the northern hemisphere) and may
end up almost parallel to the coast.

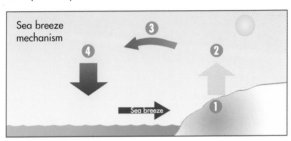

Sea breeze mechanism

Sea breeze mechanism

1 The air over the land is warmed and expands.
   A rise of 1^{0}C to 2^{0}C over sea temperature is sufficient.
2 This causes an excess of air (an imbalance of pressure)
   at some higher level, usually between 300 and 1000 m.
3 Air flows out seawards to remove the imbalance, helped
   by the offshore gradient wind.
4 Air moves downwards (subsides) over the sea to take the
   place of air which is beginning to move across the shore.

Land breezes - breezes blowing seawards from the land - are less
significant, and can occur in clear weather at night or in the early
morning. They may extend only a couple of miles out to sea, and
their strength depends on the contours of the land; the steeper the
coast the stronger the breeze. The cause is the cooling of land at
night. The air over it is cooled, becomes denser and 'drains' out
to sea down valleys.

THE BAROMETER

There should be an aneroid barometer aboard every boat.
A barometer records the local atmospheric pressure, but it is the
way it moves - rising, falling, or steady - that is of most concern,
which is the reason for noting its readings regularly in the log.
Nevertheless, a barometer's actual reading should be checked by
comparison with a reading from the local Met. office.

- In general a falling barometer indicates worsening weather,
  a rise indicates improvement.
- A falling barometer combined with backing winds are
  a reliable sign of strong winds and an approaching low.
- *Long foretold, long last - short notice, soon past.* Major weather
  changes are often heralded by gradual rising or falling.
  Sudden falls are often warnings of short, sharp blows.
- *Rise after low, foretells stronger blow.* When a cold front passes
  the pressure rises and the wind increases for an hour or so.

FOG

Radiation fog forms over the land when the land cools.
It may drift out over the sea, but does not usually travel far.
If the forecast is for the fog to clear ashore, it is likely also to
clear at sea.

Advection or Sea fog is caused by warm tropical maritime
air blowing in over cold water, eg south-westerlies (UK).
Although fog is of great concern to the sailor it is not generally
something than he can easily forecast for himself. In summer
and autumn sea fog is most frequent out to sea; in spring and
winter it occurs inshore. It can persist even in strong winds and
will continue until the tropical air mass is replaced.

RECORDING THE SHIPPING FORECAST AND DRAWING A WEATHER MAP.

It is recommended that you use RYA/R.Met.Soc 'Metmaps',
available in pads from chandlers.

Symbols and abbreviations
When taking down information from the Shipping Forecast some
sort of shorthand is needed and it is best to use the Beaufort
letters. There are also plotting symbols, but it is easier to use
the letters, which are generally self-evident.

r rain; d drizzle; s snow; p showers; h hail; th thunder;
q squall; m mist; f fog; z haze. Where appropriate a capital can
be used; eg R heavy rain. Continuous rain can be written as rr.

General synopsis
Use H and L for Highs and Lows, / for passage of time, and any
convenient abbreviation for Sea Areas. Thus 'Depression 982 mb
over Fastnet at 1200 today is expected over Dogger 992 mb at
1200 tomorrow' could be written down as L Fas 982/Dog 992'.

Sea area forecasts
'SW gale 8, veering NW and decreasing 5 to 6' can be:
SW 8/NW 5-6.

Visibility
g - good, m - moderate, p - poor.

Barometric pressure
Last two figures will suffice - write 995 as 95, 1005 as 05.

Time basis for your map

Draw the map for the same time as station reports are issued.

Times - all in Local Time (not UT)

Issued at	Broadcast at	Gen Synopsis at	Coast Stn Rept at	Draw Chart at
0000	0048	1900	2300	2300
0500	0535	0100	0400	0400
1100	1201	0700	1000	1000
1700	1754	1300	1600	1600

There are two stages in making the map:
(a) Recording the information. This is no problem using the Metmap layout and the abbreviations suggested above.
(b) Plotting the information and drawing in the isobars.
When plotting wind directions and strengths, either from station reports or as forecast, use symbols. Winds are shown as feathered arrows, with the feathers on the clockwise side of the arrow. One feather shows Force 2, one and a half is Force 3 and so on.

If the wind force or direction is forecast to change, it is best to show either the higher value or the mean, so that 'NW4 increasing to 6' can be plotted as 5 or 6.

northwest 4 to 5, showers, good.

There is no need to draw a map to cover the whole area. From about 200 miles upwind to 100 miles downwind will usually suffice.

Plotting
1 Plot the pressure and wind at each coastal station position (and include your own).
2 Plot the position of any highs or lows given in the synopsis. This means interpolating their position and values between the time of the synopsis (usually 4 - 6 hours earlier) and the end time (usually 19 or 20 hours later than the time of the observations). Also sketch in any troughs or ridges if they are given.
3 Plot predicted wind speed and direction and weather in each forecast area.

You now have a significant amount of wind information and pressure values on your chart. Try to sketch in the isobars to fit the pressure values. Align the isobars so that the wind is blowing along them but slightly towards the centre of the low, and remembering that the stronger the wind, the closer the isobars. Use standard values for the isobars, starting at 1000 mb and using 4 mb intervals (2mb in light weather).

UK SEA AREAS

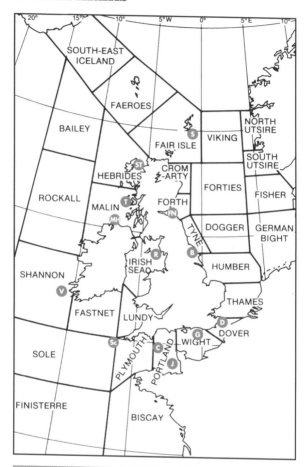

Coastal Reports

Tiree	**T**	Jersey	**J**
Stornaway	**ST**	Channel LV Auto	**C**
Sumburgh	**S**	Scilly Auto	**Sc**
Fife Ness	**FN**	Valentia	**V**
Bridlington	**B**	Ronaldsway	**R**
Dover	**D**	Malin Head	**MH**
Greenwich LV Auto	**G**		

6 Flags

FLAG ETIQUETTE

Ensign

- The owner's national maritime flag.
- Hoist 0800 (0900 in winter) if on board.
- Lower at sunset or 2100 (whichever is earlier).
- Lower when racing.
- Lower when crew ashore (unless temporarily).
- Ensigns are normally worn from an ensign staff at the stern. In a yawl or ketch they may be worn at the mizzen masthead.

Dipping the ensign

- Dip the ensign (not the burgee) to a royal yacht or any warship.
1. Dip the ensign.
2. Wait for a dip and re-hoist.
3. Re-hoist the ensign.

Special ensigns

eg blue ensign
- A warrant must be carried on board.
- Flown only when the owner is on board or near by.
- At the same time, fly the burgee of the warranted club.

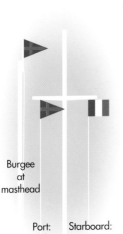
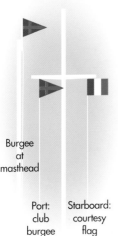

Burgee at masthead

Port: club burgee

Starboard: courtesy flag

Burgee

- Flying a club burgee indicates that the person in charge of the yacht is a member of that club. Not more than one club burgee should be flown at the same time and a burgee is not flown when racing.

Burgees should be flown from a burgee stick at the main masthead, but the number of masthead instruments now often makes this difficult, and the burgee may then be flown at the starboard crosstree.
- Lower at night, with the ensign.

Courtesy flag

- Any yacht visiting a foreign harbour should fly the marine ensign of that country at the starboard crosstrees, but not inferior to any other flag. This may mean you fly the club burgee from the port crosstrees.

INTERNATIONAL CODE FLAGS, MORSE CODE

 A Alpha
• —

 B Bravo
— • • •

 C Charlie
— • — •

 D Delta
— • •

 E Echo
•

 F Foxtrot
• • — •

 G Golf
— — •

 H Hotel
• • • •

 I India
• •

 J Juliet
• — — —

 K Kilo
— • —

 L Lima
• — • •

 M Mike
— —

 N November
— •

 O Oscar
— — —

 P Papa
• — — •

 Q Quebec
— — • —

 R Romeo
• — •

 S Sierra
• • •

 T Tango
—

 U Uniform
• • —

 V Victor
• • • —

 W Whiskey
• — —

 X X-ray
— • • —

 Y Yankee
— • — —

 Z Zulu
— — • •

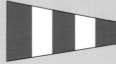 Code and answering pendant

FLAGS

NUMERAL PENDANTS AND SUBSTITUTES

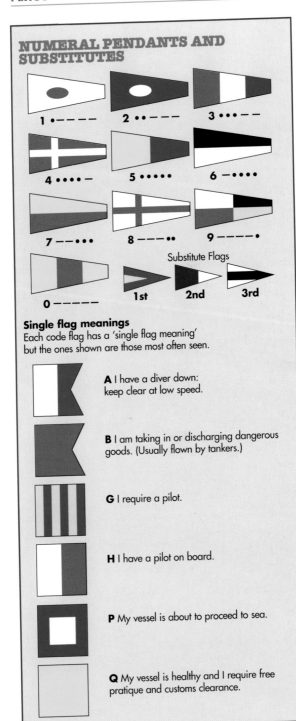

1 •———

2 ••——

3 •••——

4 ••••—

5 •••••

6 —••••

7 ——•••

8 ———••

9 ————•

0 —————

Substitute Flags

1st

2nd

3rd

Single flag meanings

Each code flag has a 'single flag meaning'
but the ones shown are those most often seen.

A I have a diver down:
keep clear at low speed.

B I am taking in or discharging dangerous
goods. (Usually flown by tankers.)

G I require a pilot.

H I have a pilot on board.

P My vessel is about to proceed to sea.

Q My vessel is healthy and I require free
pratique and customs clearance.

7 Seamanship

ANCHORING

Recommended anchor and chain sizes

Boat length metres/feet	CQR weight in pounds (will vary for other types of anchor)						
	15	20	25	35	45	60	75
8m / 26ft							
10m / 32.5ft							
12m / 39ft							
14m / 45.5ft							
16m / 52ft							
18m / 58.5ft							
20m / 65ft							
22m / 71.5 ft							
Reccomended chain size	1/4" (6mm)	5/16" (8mm)	5/16" (8mm)	5/16" (8mm)	3/8" (10mm)	3/8" (10mm)	1/2" (12mm)
CQR Weights lb/kg	15lb (6.8kg)	20lb (9.1kg)	25lb (11.3kg)	35lb (15.9kg)	45lb (20.4kg)	60lb (27.2kg)	70lb (34kg)

If your boat has a heavy displacement, use the next size up.
* Chain is preferable to rope.
* If you must use warp, have at least 5 m of chain between warp and anchor. This prevents chafe, and allows a more horizontal pull on the anchor.
* Always have two anchors on board.

How much cable?
* Work out the maximum depth of water you expect (d)
* Put out at least 4d for chain and 6d for rope in calm conditions, and a lot more if rough.

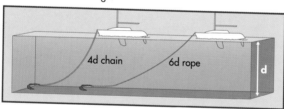

4d chain   6d rope   d

Anchor gear
* If you're using rope, nylon is best because it stretches.

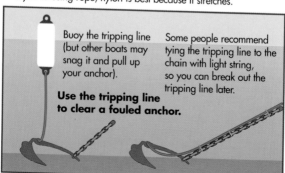

Buoy the tripping line (but other boats may snag it and pull up your anchor).

Some people recommend tying the tripping line to the chain with light string, so you can break out the tripping line later.

Use the tripping line to clear a fouled anchor.

- Have a length of (split) polythene tubing to protect the rope through the bow roller.
- Make sure the bow roller runs freely, and there is a pin across.
- Mouse the anchor shackle so it can't come undone.
- Mark the chain and/or warp so you can see how much has been let go.
- Secure the inboard end - but in such a way that it can be slipped or cut in an emergency.
- Fit a tripping line if you're afraid the anchor will foul.

Where to anchor

- Good holding ground. Look at the chart and consult the pilot book. Sand (S) mud (M) and clay (Cy) are best. A rocky bottom (R) is to be avoided and weed (Wd) gives unreliably holding.
- Good shelter from wind and sea, taking careful note of any forecast change in wind direction. Clear of a strong tidal stream. Adequate swinging room, which is not easy to judge in a crowded anchorage. A nearby boat riding to an anchor warp will range through a larger circle than one riding on chain. Any boat coming to anchor must keep clear of other craft already at anchor and try to avoid the risk of picking up another boat's anchor gear.
- Sufficient depth of water. Shallow water means less anchor cable needed, but there must be enough depth at low water - with a safety margin. This includes the area where the boat may swing when the tide changes.
- Avoid anchoring where the bottom shelves steeply - if you drag into deep water, the anchor will be pulled up!
- Keep out of busy channels.

How to anchor

- Flake the required length of cable on deck.
- Prepare the anchor for letting go when the order comes.
- Under engine, approach into the tide (or wind, if this is stronger).
- Under sail, approach on a close reach.
- Stop, then let go.
- Kick the engine astern, to lay out the cable.

Transit, to check for dragging

- Check (stop) the cable to help the anchor dig in.
- Motor astern to dig it in fully.
- Take a transit to check for dragging.
  Alternatively, take bearings of 2 or 3 objects on the shore.
- Secure the anchor cable round both cleats on the foredeck.

Anchor wrinkles

- If the anchor is fouled, you may be able to motor over it (taking in the slack) and break it out. If you are sailing off, tack one way then the other.
- If the anchor is snatching in waves, put out a good length of chain plus 10 - 20 metres of nylon rope as a shock-absorber. Alternatively, lower a weight halfway down the anchor chain.

Anchor snagged on a cable

- If you snag a cable, pull
  up the anchor.
- Slip a rope around
  the cable, and make fast.
- Drop the anchor until clear,
  then retrieve it.
- Finally, release the cable.

Using two anchors

The Fork Moor is useful for added
security, especially in a strong blow.
It also reduces yawing.

1 Drop first anchor. If one of your
cables is rope and chain, use that first.

2 Motor to where second anchor
is to be dropped, and let go.
Line between anchors should be at right angles to direction
of wind. Easier to judge if first anchor is buoyed.

3 Drop back, while adjusting both cables so that strain is equal.
Angle between cables should
be about 45 degrees.

The Bahamian Moor is useful to
reduce swinging room in a
crowded anchorage, and in an
area where a tide flows
through the anchorage.

1 Drop the main anchor first.
Go astern, paying out twice
the normal amount of cable.

2 Let go the second anchor.
Pay out its cable while
heaving in on the first
anchor until the boat
is centred.

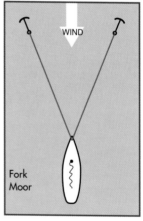

WIND

Fork
Moor

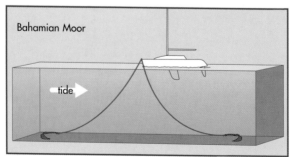

Bahamian Moor

tide

KNOTS AND WHIPPING

Round turn & two half hitches. Attaching a rope to a post.

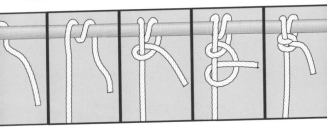

Clove hitch. Attaching a rope to a ring or post.

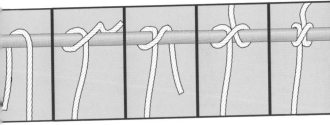

Figure of eight. As a stopper.

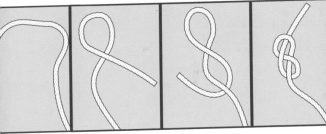

Reef knot. For tying the ends of a rope around an object, eg a reef.

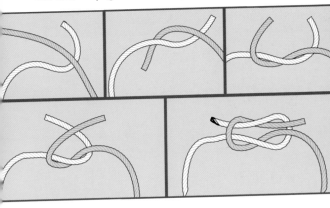

Bowline. Making a secure loop in a rope.

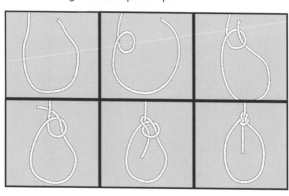

Sheet bend. Joining two ropes of similar thickness.

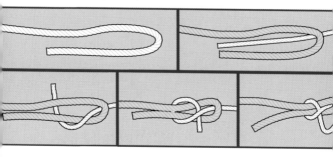

Rolling hitch. To attach a line to a rod or another rope so it grips it.

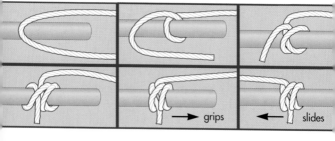

Whipping

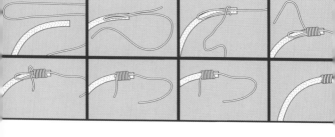

LOOKING AFTER THE HULL

- Seacocks must move freely. If stiff, strip and refit when the boat is hauled out.
- No corrosion, and pipe secured with double stainless steel hose clamps.
- Have a softwood bung adjacent.

thickness of hull

Cockpit drains

- Sited so that the cockpit will empty on either tack, and the hull openings must be fitted with seacocks. Drains are often too small.
- Fill the cockpit to see how quickly it drains.

The target is 2-3 minutes, which seems a long time when the cockpit is full of water.

The RORC Regulations now require boats over 8.5m to have 4 x 20 mm diameter drains.

Steering gear

- Inspect rudder fastenings whenever the boat is hauled out.
- Rods or cables joining a wheel to the rudder head will usually be concealed, but annually they should be opened up, inspected for wear and lubricated.
- Inspect the steering quadrant's stops inside the hull. If worn, the quadrant may ride over them and jam.
- Try out the emergency tiller to ensure that it does fit and the crew know how to use it.

Hauling out checklist

- Seacocks. Check these before the boat comes out in case any need refitting.
- Water intakes (toilets, engine cooling). Ensure that any strainers are clean and clear.
- Sacrificial zinc anodes. Renew any that are badly wasted.
- Depth finder. Clean off the external transducer in the hull. Normally this will not be antifouled.
- Log/speedometer. Withdraw any retractable fittings and take care others are not damaged.
- Rudder fittings. Inspect carefully and check for excessive play.
- Stern gland and shaft bearing. If gland has been leaking excessively and re-packing seems necessary, this is the time to do it.

NOTE: Rudder fittings and the shaft are two areas where expert advice is always valuable.

- Propeller. Inspect for signs of damage.

FITTING OUT

This checklist refers to the ultimate part of fitting out - ensuring that after the work is completed, the boat is ready to sail.

GENERAL
* Insurance policy covers new period afloat and start of active cruising.
* All gear landed for storage has returned on board.
* Check bilges clear of rubbish. Test bilge pumps. The only effective test of a bilge pump is that it does actually pump water out of the bilge and over the side. If in doubt put water in the bilge and try.
* Test steering gear. See rudder post is not leaking, and no gear likely to foul it.
* Fill fresh water tanks, test pumps and look out for leaks.
* Sight all safety and emergency equipment and see it is properly stowed.
* Test VHF with another station.

ENGINE TRIAL.
* Run engine at idle and then in gear alongside. Carry out routine pre-sailing check. (See page 101.)

NAVIGATION etc.
* Check compass - initially comparison with hand bearing compass will do, then with a transit when possible.
* Test compass light and navigation lights.
* Check charts aboard. Get new almanac - throw away old.
* Test GPS or other electronic nav. equipment.
* Test echo sounder.

ON DECK
* Check clutch and brakes on anchor windlass.
* Look at anchor shackles. Renew mousing if needed.
* Dinghy - check equipment and if inflatable, test for leaks.
* De-winterise outboard motor and test.

Hurrying off to sea after a refit or lay-up is often the cause of trouble because the boat's gear has not been properly checked out. Better to plan a short outing first, before starting a longer passage. Then there is a chance to put things right if anything is found to be missing or not working well.

LAYING UP

* During the last cruise of the season try to check out every part of the boat - pumps, winches, electronics. Look carefully at every sail and item of rigging. Then make a really comprehensive work list. Sub-divide into:
  - jobs for the owner or crew
  - yard or outside work
  - items for purchase or renewal.
* Arrange any work to be done be mechanics, yards, sailmakers, etc. as soon as the boat is laid up. In the case of a winter lay-up the spring rush will be avoided.

Laying up checklist

GENERAL
- Diesel tank. Fill (unless there is reason otherwise) to reduce chance of condensation.
- Insurance. Check that boat is covered for being laid up, and for any gear taken home or stowed elsewhere.
- Gear removed from boat: make an inventory showing where it is stowed, taken for repair etc.
- Portable valuables: remove binoculars, watches, radios etc, unless they are quite secure on board.
- Bottled gas & outboard fuel: remove
- Water tanks. Empty. Before next season flush through with Puraclean (or similar).
- Toilets: Flush through thoroughly, then close seacocks and winterise according to maker's instructions. Stripping and refitting is usually advised.

MAST AND STANDING RIGGING
- Mast: If it is to be unstepped:
  - electrical leads tallied to ensure easy reconnecting
  - standing rigging labelled before taking off mast
  - mast and spars marked with boat's name before stowing ashore. Many masts look the same!

ELECTRICAL
- Batteries: Unless they are to be kept on charge aboard, remove ashore for care, marked with boat's name.
- Dry batteries: Remove from flashlights, radios, buoyant lights, and any other equipment. Spray battery connections with WD40 or similar.

SAILS AND RUNNING RIGGING
- Send sails to sailmaker for repairs and/or laundry.
- Unreeve running rigging, check for wear, label and stow.
- Unrig self-furling gear and follow maker's instructions for seasonal maintenance.

ENGINE
- Close sea water intake (make sure engine cannot be started). If needed, flush cooling water system with fresh water, drain and winterise according to maker's instructions.
- Check recommended maintenance schedule. Regardless of hours run it is sensible to change engine oil and filter and fuel filters during lay up.

EMERGENCY EQUIPMENT
- Send liferaft for servicing if needed.
- Inspect lifejackets and service if needed.
- Stow flares in dry place away from fire risk. Check expiry date.
- Take medical kit home for overhaul.

DOMESTIC
- Remove ALL food, including dry provisions and canned goods.
- Empty icebox, scrub out with disinfectant and leave open.
- Scrub out toilet and shower compartment with disinfectant (to help reduce mildew)
- Launder sleeping bags, towels etc.
- Remove all those items that accumulate in almost any boat - odd bits of clothing, old magazines, etc.

Engine failure is the most common cause of Coastguard incidents per year, and the reason for over a thousand lifeboat launchings to assist yachts and other pleasure craft, some of which had merely run out of fuel.

So there are two clear aims for a skipper:

1 Trying to prevent breakdowns by regular engine maintenance - including pre-sailing checks.
2 Being able to deal with a minor breakdown, if it should occur - especially at sea.

MAINTENANCE

Accessibility

Before thinking about maintaining or repairing an engine, it is essential to identify the key parts - and be able to get at them. This is not always as easy as it should be, but engine accessibility has improved in modern designs. These are the essentials:

A seacock and filter for seawater inlet

B fuel cut-off valve

C primary fuel filter (for draining and changing the element)

D fuel pump (for priming the system manually)

E engine oil dip-stick

F gearbox oil dip-stick

G engine oil filter (for changing the element)

H secondary fuel filter

I sea water pump (for changing the impeller)

J propeller shaft stern gland

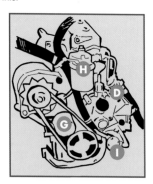

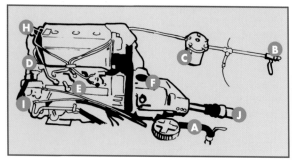

- Most skippers will have no problems with this list, but it is always worthwhile checking that these items can be identified and are accessible.

Pre-sailing checks

- A regular pre-sailing check is a part of proper maintenance. It is poor seamanship to leave the security of a marina or mooring without spending a few minutes to make sure - as far as possible - that the engine is running properly. The fact that it was doing so last weekend (or yesterday) is no guarantee. *And the longer it is since the boat was last used, the more careful the pre-sailing check needs to be.*

The engine manual will advise, but this is a useful guide:

Engine pre-sailing check

Fuel
- Check visually that there is at least enough fuel for the intended voyage, and carry an emergency supply.

Engine
- Open the engine compartment and look around. Any oil or water leaks, or loose wires? Are the belts sound and tight?
- Is the seawater inlet valve open, and the strainer clear?
- Check the engine oil level with the dipstick. Do not overfill.
- Check the fresh water level in the header tank.
- Check the fuel pre-filter and drain any water.
- Petrol engine: operate the engine space exhaust fan.
- Put the gearbox in neutral, start the engine, and run it at medium revs to warm it up.
- Check the ahead/astern operation, cooling water discharge, oil pressure, and that the batteries are being charged.
- Stern gland. Check this periodically for leaks while the engine is running. Tighten the grease filler (if fitted) as required.

Gearbox oil.
Check this weekly when the engine is running and is warm.

At sea.
Keep an eye on the instruments (oil pressure, temperature, battery charging). Have a regular look inside the engine compartment when the engine is running. This is the time, for example, when a cooling water leak may be spotted.

A clean engine compartment makes it much easier to spot corrosion, leaks or other defects.

TROUBLESHOOTING AND REPAIRS

Engine will not start

PROBLEM: Starter motor will not turn or turns too slowly to start engine.

1 Check battery with voltmeter.
- Try other battery - or both batteries together.
- Try starting with decompression lever engaged, closing it when the engine is turning OK.

> One fully charged battery must always be kept for starting, which is the most important job a battery has to do.

2 Check that connections to battery terminals are clean and really tight.
3 Check there are no loose wiring connections to starter motor, starter switch, and battery selection switch.
4 Try hand start, with decompression lever engaged until the engine turns over.

PROBLEM: Starter motor turns engine, but engine will not start. Do not run battery flat.

1 Check there is fuel in tank and fuel isolation switch is open.
   NOTE: If fuel tank is ever refilled after being empty, it may be necessary to bleed fuel system. (See below.)
2 Check engine stop valve is open. Cable operated valves may stick, and electrically operated valves may jam in the closed position.
3 Maybe air in fuel (most likely cause of non-starting). Check for loose connections in fuel lines.
4 Bleed fuel system. (See below.)

Bleeding the fuel system

This operation is needed to remove air from the fuel system, which may be caused by a leak in the fuel lines. Bleeding is also required after changing fuel filters, after any other work on the fuel system and after running out of fuel.

• Knowing how to bleed a diesel engine is simple but essential knowledge, and might have to be done at sea. If in doubt, get instruction from a mechanic before going to sea.

The 'bleeding points' may vary and will be shown in the engine manual.

1 Identify bleed screw and slacken off. Normally this is on the fine filter housing (A).
2 Work hand priming lever on fuel lift pump (B).

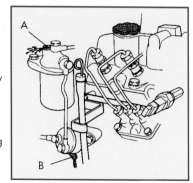

3 If fuel coming from vent contains bubbles it is a sign of air in system. Continue pumping until clear fuel flows out with no bubbles. Tighten screw while continuing to operate lift pump.

4 No fuel comes from vent. Primary fuel filter (C) may be blocked. Close the fuel cock at the tank. Clean out filter, replace element, open the fuel cock, then complete bleeding as in 3. above.

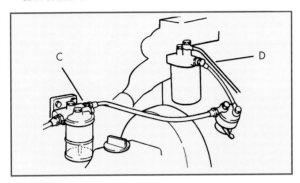

5 After replacing pre-filter, fuel still does not flow. Replace element in fine filter (D) and repeat operation

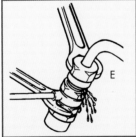

6 Clear fuel comes from vent. But, after tightening vent, engine still does not start. Slacken high pressure line to one injector (E), turn over engine until fuel flows without bubbles.

In practice, bleeding the fuel system is usually successful after step 3.

Remember: There are two basic requirements:

1 Fuel must clearly be able to pass through both filters.

2 The fuel system must be completely free of air.

Engine overheating

Many engines have an alarm that sounds if the engine overheats.
Further evidence will be the temperature gauge on the instrument
panel, and no cooling water flowing from the exhaust. Overheating
will not stop an engine from starting or running but will rapidly
cause engine damage.

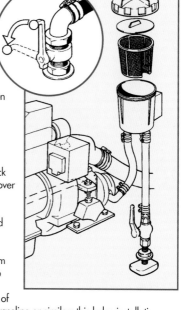

1 Stop the engine
2 Check sea water
   intake is clear:
   - Close seacock
   on intake
   - Open filter and
   remove any debris.
   (Plastic bags can
   block water intakes,
   but may float free when
   engine is stopped.)
3 Is sea water pump
   impeller damaged?
   Usual indication is hot
   cover plate on pump.
   - Close the inlet seacock
   - Unscrew the pump cover
   plate (keep the screws
   carefully)
   - Remove the damaged
   impeller (see diagram)
   - Take great care to
   remove any debris from
   the system in the pump
   inlet and outlet.
   - Wipe over the blade of
the new impeller with vaseline or similar; this helps installation
- Insert new impeller (a clockwise rotating movement helps) and
replace cover plate. Alternatively, compress the blades with a
jubilee clip 'half on', (or tie a piece of string to hold them tight).
Insert half way, slip off the clip, then push home. Make sure the
gasket is replaced before fitting the cover.

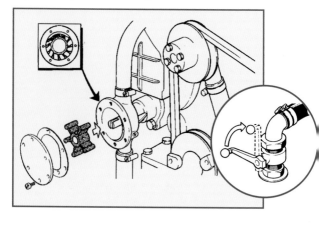

Running out of fuel

- **Don't!**
- Check that your fuel gauge is accurate.
- Stow spare diesel fuel.
- Know your fuel consumption.
- Cruise at the economical speed.

TOOLS AND SPARES

Set of spanners/wrenches - imperial and/or metric (according to engine). Combined open ended/ring spanners are best, preferably with slim jaws to ease access to difficult nuts and bolts.

Adjustable spanners - 3 sizes	'Allen' (hexagonal) key set
Mole grips	Slip joint pliers
Electrical wire strippers	Screwdrivers - 3 sizes
Crosshead screwdrivers	Stub screwdriver
Midget screwdriver (electrical work)	
Right-angled screwdrivers	Electrical pliers
Needle nosed pliers	Hammer
Cold chisel	Punch
Hacksaw and blades	Files, round and flat
Hand drill and drill set	

Socket set (not essential but very useful for engine work)
Spanner to fit the stern gland (can be large and an unusual size)
Strap wrench (for undoing filters)

Engine spares Also consult handbook or local agent.
A larger kit is needed for extended cruising.

Two water pump impellers and gaskets
An element for fuel pre-filter
A fuel fine filter element
Sufficient lubricating oil to refill engine
Fuel lift pump repair kit or complete pump
Spare belts for water pump and alternator.

- There are types and sizes of engine spare (eg belts and impellers) that look similar. When ordering spares it is important to quote the serial number.

General maintenance gear
Selection of hose clamps.
Plastic tubing (various sizes)
Self amalgamating repair tape
Electrical tape
Selection of electrical terminals
WD40 or similar
Petroleum jelly
Stern tube packing (if appropriate) Check the size.

9 Skippering

CREW BRIEFING

Aboard any boat at any time it is potentially dangerous if the skipper is the only person who knows where the emergency equipment is stowed and what to do if anything goes wrong.

Which means than any new crew should be fully briefed about safety and how to deal with emergencies.

One practical solution is for the boat to have a Safety Card in the style shown below with the individual details for the boat completed. The card is kept as a permanent reminder near the chart table, and a copy shown to each crew member to read. This arrangement may, in fact, be more effective than a hurried verbal briefing.

SUGGESTED SAFETY CARD

Yacht.............................

Safety on board
In any boat all the crew must know how to avoid accidents
- and what to do if anything does go wrong.

The Stove: Please locate gas bottle stowage and turn off
at bottle after use.
- Do not use a gas lighter for stove or oven.
- Even in calm weather take care, when pouring out a hot drink, not to scald your feet and legs. Use oilskin trousers at the stove in bumpy weather.
- Note the *Fire Blanket* stowage and use it for any stove fire.

Heads: How to operate.

Safety Harnesses: Except for a short sail, everyone will have a personal harness allocated. Adjust yours to fit, and stow it with your gear. Wear it: - always on deck at night - in rough weather and if the skipper asks you to. Also whenever you may feel more confident wearing it (there is nothing soft in being safe).
But a harness is no good unless it is clipped on.
Look around the deck and know where to clip on.

On deck: <u>Reefing</u> can be essential for comfortable sailing, but in a blow it could be essential for safety.
Roller furling jib - not much problem
Mainsail furling - usually simple, but <u>all the crew should find out how it works *in advance.*</u>

The engine: Know how to start it (but <u>only</u> do so if asked by the skipper). *Before starting ALWAYS look for any lines over the side that might get caught in the propeller!*

Letting go the anchor: Not often needed in a hurry, but something all the crew should know.

Life jackets: Stowage...
May sometimes be allocated individually.

Fire extinguishers: Stowage..................................
Look at the instructions - absolutely no time to read them if there is a fire.

Medical/first aid kit: Stowage.............................
Minor 'ready to use' items.......................................

Flares for getting help in an emergency
Stowage...

VHF distress calls
In an emergency VHF radio is the best way to get help, and may have to be used by someone with no radio experience. Emergency operating instructions are by the radio.

Bilge pumps Not only used in an emergency.
Pump (1) position ....
suction (1) ....
Pump (2) position ....
suction (2) ....
If a pump gets blocked, it can be cleared by removing any debris from the strainer on the suction.

Man overboard gear:
All crew must know the Man Overboard gear available - lifebuoys, buoyant lights etc - and *how to use it*.

MOB button on GPS (if fitted):
Crew must know where it is and how to use it.

Liferaft (when carried):
Know where it is stowed and how to launch.

Crew clothing
- Make sure inexperienced crews know what to bring.
- Be firm: ensure warm clothing and foul weather gear are put on in good time.

SEASICKNESS/EXHAUSTION
Before starting, ask yourself:
1 How long - reasonably - is the passage going to take? Are there any bolt-holes available?
2 Is it going to be rough? What is the forecast? In spring and autumn risk of poor weather is higher than in summer.
3 Are the crew liable to be sick? Do you really know - have you sailed with them before on a long passage? (Being short-handed needs a stronger crew.)
4 Are we simply trying to be 'back for work on Monday?'
5 Can we cope, or are we taking chances.
  SO, SHOULD WE GO ON?

PREPARING FOR SEA

This must be an inevitable routine in fair weather and foul.
While the skipper is ultimately responsible, the crew must feel
that they are very much part of the act.
- Hatches and ports tightly secured.
- Loose gear below decks stowed away, lockers latched shut.
- Galley gear given special check.
- Dinghy - towing line checked if to be towed.
  Securely lashed if carried on deck.
- Dinghy oars, fenders, warps, and all loose deck gear
  either stowed below or lashed on deck.
- Liferaft lashed securely.
- Anchor ready.
- No warps overboard.

WATCHES AND NIGHT PASSAGES

Normally a system of watches should be set up for a night passage,
and even for a long day passage. And watches should be started
soon after leaving harbour, otherwise there is a risk of all the crew
becoming tired at the same time, despite the protestations of "I'll be
OK, I don't need any sleep".
- Most importantly the skipper should consider himself. The end
  of the passage is likely to involve a landfall and maybe the
  entry into a strange harbour - a time when the skipper should
  be reasonably rested and thinking clearly.
- The best arrangement and the length of watches must depend
  on the number and strength of the crew, and on the weather.
  Longer watches allow more sleep for those off watch, but in
  bad weather and on a short passage, shorter watches (eg two
  hours) may be better.

Two	A	2000 – 2300	
Watch	B	2300 – 0200	
Keepers	A	0200 – 0500	etc
Three	A	2000 – 2200	
Watch	B	2200 – 2400	
Keepers	C	2400 – 0200	etc

- For a night passage the skipper must be absolutely firm about
  the safety arrangements. Helmsman and any other crew in the
  cockpit must wear harnesses, and the rule about never leaving
  the cockpit (unless to go below) must be rigidly enforced.
  If something like reefing has to be done this should be under
  the skipper's supervision.

- Other points:
- There must be a powerful torch in the cockpit in case of another
  vessel coming too close. Some skippers will also like to have a white
  flare on hand.
- Cabin lighting must not blind crew on deck. Torches may be used
  for dressing, making drinks, and at the chart table.

PAPERWORK

Registration

A yacht used solely in British waters does not have to be registered, but when cruising abroad, authorities will almost certainly demand the 'ship's papers' and registration is recommended.

There are two types of registration: Part 1 and Part 3, (referring to the Merchant Shipping Registration Regulations of 1993). Part 3 is the Small Ship Register (SSR).

Whereas Part I registration can be complicated and expensive, entry on the SSR costs only a few pounds for five years registration.

A yacht may be registered on the SSR if she is under 24 m (79 ft) and owned by a British or Commonwealth citizen who is 'ordinarily resident in the UK'. Yachts owned by companies have to be entered in Part I and also those under a marine mortgage.

Further information on both types of registration, and copies of Registry forms are available from Registry of Shipping and Seamen, PO Box 165, Cardiff CF14 5FU. Tel. 02920 768211.

International Certificate of Competence (ICC) for pleasure craft

Most foreign countries now insist on proof of skippers' competence to sail. The RYA operate the DOT system for the UK. This consists of a two-hour practical test which can be taken on your own boat. Phone the RYA on 02380 627400 for a list of authorised examiners.

Radio licences

It is illegal to operate a radio aboard, including a VHF and portable VHF, without a **Ship Radio Licence**. This can be obtained from: Radio Licensing Centre, PO Box 1495, Bristol, BS99 3QS. Tel: 0870 243 4433.

The licence must be displayed in a window, as in a car, and preferably on the port side. This licence is not transferable, and if the boat is sold details of the new owner should be sent to Wray Castle. Using a radio without a licence can incur a fine.

Certificate of Competence (Operator's licence). Anyone using a marine R/T, including VHF, should be an authorised operator who has qualified for the Certificate of Competence. This is administered by the RYA who offer short courses, arrange the examinations, and issue the cerificates. Details from RYA, RYA House, Romsey Road, Eastleigh, Hants SO5 4YB. Tel: 02920 627400.

In fact a radio may be used by anyone, provided they are closely supervised by an authorised operator, which essentially means there must be an authorised operator in every crew.

VICTUALLING AND FEEDING

 If there is someone in the crew who is experienced and takes charge of the feeding, the skipper is lucky and has one less thing to think about. But he is still ultimately responsible - as he is for everything else aboard - and there are times when he may have to intervene.

- An indigestible and greasy supper is not the right prelude to a night passage with an uncertain crew. And while a good fry-up breakfast may be welcome on most days, maybe not if the day's sail looks like being choppy.
- Under good conditions most crews have a good appetite and, apart from meals, a supply of hot drinks and snacks is good for morale, especially during a night passage.
- In bad weather, a hot drink and some sort of food, (crude sandwiches, biscuits, chocolate, fruit, etc) are essential for crew morale. Food can be prepared in advance and hot drinks can be put in a thermos, but the galley should also be organised so that a hot drink can be brewed in bumpy weather. Soup or Bovril/Oxo may be more digestible than tea or coffee.
- The skipper must ensure that there are always reasonable emergency supplies aboard in case of a delayed arrival in harbour. This particularly applies to longer passages.

BEHAVIOUR AND COURTESY

The RYA skipper's syllabus requires an understanding of the 'ordinary practice of seamen and yachtsmen', not only with the use of burgees and ensigns, but 'the prevention of unnecessary noise or disturbance in harbour including courtesies to other craft berthed alongside'.

Less experienced crews may sometimes need a gentle reminder about this, which can apply equally when alongside a dock or marina, or in an anchorage.
- Noise can be a major aggravation to others, so no loud music at any time, especially late at night.
- Returning from a cheerful run ashore, there is no reason for the crew to share their exuberance with others.
- When berthing alongside other yachts, the outside boat should always put a line ashore fore and aft if possible.
- Always cross quietly any boat alongside, via the foredeck (without peering down the forehatch!) and never across the cockpit.
- With several boats berthed alongside each other, an inside boat needing to make an early start should warn the others, and can possibly move to the outside on the previous evening.
- Whether there is anyone aboard or not, halyards must always be left tied so that they do not slat.

CUSTOMS REGULATIONS

When a boat sails to or from the UK it is the skipper's responsibility to see that customs regulations are obeyed. These regulations are contained in Customs Notice 8 which is available from any HM Customs and Excise office.

Lifeboats
Offshore

"As sailors, we can always count on volunteer lifeboat crews. Can they count on you? Please join *Offshore* today."

Sir Robin Knox-Johnston CBE, RD

However experienced you are at sea, you never know when you'll need the help of a lifeboat crew. But to keep saving lives, the Royal National Lifeboat Institution's volunteer crews need your help.

That is why you should join Offshore. For just £3.50 per month, you can help save thousands of lives, receive practical information to help keep you safe at sea and save money on equipment for your boat.

Please join *Offshore* – today

Call free
0800 543 210
Because life's not all plain sailing

Index